THE MEET THE PARENTS STORY:

THE MEET THE PARENTS STORY:

The true and terrible tale of how a little independent film spawned a billion-dollar franchise!

LAURA ENRIGHT

BearManor Media

2025

The Meet the Parents Story:
The true and terrible tale of how a little independent film
spawned a billion-dollar franchise!

Copyright © 2025 Laura Enright

Published in the United States of America by:

BearManor Media

1317 Edgewater Dr. #110
Orlando, FL 32804

bearmanormedia.com

Printed in the United States.

Typesetting and layout by PKJ Passion Global

ISBN–979-8-88771-648-0

Foreword

I first saw *Meet the Parents* in 1992 when it played at the Music Box Theatre on Southport Avenue in Chicago. I read in the paper that Greg Glienna, an old friend from high school, had made an independent film and it was going to run for a few weeks at the historic theater, so I gathered some friends, and we went to see the film. We enjoyed the dark comedy so much that we went for a second viewing when it was shown at another theater.

My first introduction to Greg Glienna came in 1981 during the Maine South High School's Variety Show in which he performed in skits between larger acts. Later I'd see him, twice, playing Professor Henry Higgins in the school's production of *My Fair Lady*. I believe it was during the second performance that he dealt with a faulty stage door so expertly that they should have incorporated the bit in future performances of the play.

I have to admit, I had a little crush on him. One of those pathetic high school crushes that you know will go nowhere but nevertheless burns brightly for the duration of the school year. I think I had about four of those forest fires burning that year, all of them unquenchable.

I hated high school. By junior year, my discomfort in high school led me to call in sick practically every Monday or Friday.

That all changed in the second semester of my junior year because that's when I looked up from the desk I chose, in the drama class my shy self for some reason decided to sign up for that semester and saw Greg Glienna walk into the room.

I never called in once the rest of my junior year.

Greg, however, was a senior at the time so our interaction was short-lived. I remember little of high school (I've tried to block it all out). But I do remember very positive interactions with Greg, who I found to be inventive and very funny. I was surprised to learn later that he was more impressed with my talent than I was at the time.

Years later, we would meet again, and I found in him a friend. A friend who apparently felt confident enough in my abilities to tell the story of his 1992 independent feature *Meet the Parents*. When Greg asked me to tell the story of *Meet the Parents,* I was both stunned and honored. Would I be able to do justice to the remarkable amount of energy and creativity that was put into making that movie? As I researched, I began to discover that while much of it is his story most certainly, and there would be no *Meet the Parents* 1992 or 2000 without him, from the beginning there were many people that helped push it forward along the way. And that there was also a remarkable amount of energy and creativity that went into the making of the 2000 remake from the moment a remake was considered. From the 1992 original to the 2000 remake, it had been a journey, and not always a pleasant one for those involved.

Hollywood has a history of both nurturing and beating the shit out of the talent that creates for you the movies you so love. Because in the end, movie making is a business and studios want to make money off of projects despite how often they're willing to lose money on projects that were nightmares to begin with. But then the latter projects are what insurance and creative accounting are for.

And so, I present to you the story of *Meet the Parents*. The true and terrible tale of how a little independent film spawned a billion-dollar franchise.

Introduction

In October 2020, the director, and four members of the cast of the 2000 mega-hit comedy *Meet the Parents* appeared on a Today Show segment in a 20th-anniversary homage to the popular film. Due to Covid restrictions, the segment was conducted via Zoom, rather than in-studio, which probably worked out great for the stars who could share their funny stories about the making of the movie from the comfort of their homes.

Viewing the show in his LA apartment, his cat Aggie curled up in his lap, screenwriter and director Greg Glienna watched as Jay Roach, Ben Stiller, Robert DeNiro, Blythe Danner, and Teri Polo recounted their experiences with the film, finding their collective backslapping during the segment more than a little frustrating. Far from being a premise unique to the creative minds behind the 2000 movie, as was implied in the interview, Universal Studios' *Meet the Parents* was simply a ramped-up remake of a movie Glienna himself co-wrote, starred in and directed almost a decade before the Universal version was made. Even the title wasn't original to Universal. It had been dreamed up by Glienna while on the bus he was taking to meet up with Mary Ruth Clark, the co-writer of the original movie. Glienna's version was also a movie that had its own fans, many of whom preferred it the remake.

The idea hadn't exactly been stolen by Universal. They bought the rights to Glienna's original movie and once the remake was complete, the studio did give "Story" credit in the titles to Glienna and Mary Ruth Clark as well as offering Glienna "Associate Producer." The problem was that having been hired by Universal to work on a script for the remake, Greg and Mary Ruth's involvement with the final script went much deeper than simply two people suggesting a "story" to studio heads. Crediting them as co-writers on the screenplay would have been a better reflection of that. Yet the only two writers listed for "Screenplay" credit are Jim Herzfeld and John Hamburg, two writers who came well after the fact, thus ensuring that Greg and Mary Ruth would never see the kind of payday that a "Screenplay" credit would bring, no matter how many of their original ideas were used.

Now, after buying the rights to the original *Meet the Parents* as part of the deal, outside of a few film festivals, Universal refuses to allow any distribution of the original, even after two decades of the remake's release.

This is perhaps understandable. *Meet the Parents* spawned two sequels, *Meet the Fockers* and *Little Fockers* and perhaps the Today Show reunion show might even have inspired a third sequel in the series, the history of which the minds at Universal would like to keep as pure as possible to their narrative.

Yet, how much of a distraction could this low-budget, independent feature made in 1992 be unless it revealed just how much of that movie could be found in the Universal version (and how questionable it was to deny Greg and Mary Ruth "Screenplay" credit)?

It can't be easy to sit and watch people feted for ideas you came up with first.

Hollywood, however, can be a jungle when it comes to creative rights and those new to the game can easily be swallowed up. As, in some respects, Greg and Mary Ruth were.

But how did *Meet the Parents* go from the five-minute short called "The Vase" which inspired Greg's 1992 movie, to the 2000 Hollywood production beloved by millions?

It starts with two young boys and their dreams of becoming film makers.

C.C. and Charlie

On a warm, sunny day in the suburb of Park Ridge, Ill., the young comedy duo of C.C. and Charlie were in the kitchen of Charlie's family trying to figure out how to film a pancake being flipped with enough flourish to stick to the ceiling. The idea of taping it to the ceiling had been considered until Charlie remembered that there were some spare ceiling tiles in a drawer and realized that they could put one on the ground and lay a pancake on it, shooting the scene down from above. A little careful editing and voila!

Quite ingenious for a couple of 10-year-olds, using a Super 8mm camera, filming in a family home in the 1970s. It is hard to imagine now when technology enables people to not only film the "movies" on cell phones but use various apps to add effects and to be able to upload them to various platforms for all to watch, but back then, even on professional productions, film making might require extra creativity when solving technical problems.

C.C.'s real name was Jim Minnice, the pseudonym was chosen because the initials rhymed with his real surname, which people had a curious problem pronouncing. Because of this, in his later career as a comic and producer, Jim would change his last name from Minnice to Vincent. For consistency's sake, we'll keep to the name Jim Vincent when referring to him.

Charlie was in actuality, Greg Glienna, his stage name chosen for no particular reason other than it worked.

Park Ridge in the 1970s and 80s was a peaceful place to grow up. About 30 minutes from downtown Chicago, it had a sizable population yet retained a small-town feel.

Glienna and Vincent met in first grade where they discovered a kinship in comedy. "I was a bit of a strange kid," Glienna admitted. "I was always drawn to old stuff. I found a record store that sold old

45s and I discovered I loved the singing of Al Jolson." Jolson was huge at the turn of the 20th century, but not quite as well known to kids who were more likely to recite the lyrics to songs by Elton John and Led Zeppelin. Every week, as Jim would excitedly rehash the latest episode of the popular police drama *Starsky & Hutch*, Greg would happily describe the guests who appeared on a variety-TV show named *Vaudeville*, hosted by Milton Berle.

While Greg was not exactly attuned to pop culture, he and Jim were on the same wavelength when it came to comedy. Laurel and Hardy, Buster Keaton, Charlie Chaplin, and many of the old-time silent movie comedians were particular inspirations for the boys. Greg especially took to heart the value of mining for comedy in particular situations and the characters' honest responses to those situations. It's a more organic style of comedy than a typical joke-filled style which often served the witticisms coming out of the character's mouth more than the character himself.

"Laurel and Hardy never had jokey jokes," Glienna explained. "I always quote this one bit they did. They're in court for vagrancy and the judge says, 'You're vagrants.' Oliver says, 'I object!' And the judge asks, 'On what grounds?' And Stanley says, 'We weren't on the grounds. We were on the park bench.' The audience in the court erupts in laughter and Stanley turns to look at them completely confused at their amusement. That's the perfect comedy. He didn't mean it to be funny."

The comedy is situational. It isn't just in Laurel's incorrect answer but also in his sincere belief that he had given the correct answer, as he understood the question, as well as his innocent reaction to the crowd's response.

Admittedly, C.C. and Charlie's pancake scene was a bit of a rip-off (or a loving homage depending on perspective) of Laurel and Hardy. The plot, as well as the film, has been lost to time (or rather to Greg's father's holding to his belief that "everything must go!" when it came time to clean out the attic where the film, as well as Greg's priceless stack of comic books, had been stored). But the boys' urge to tell stories followed them into Maine South High School where C.C. and Charlie, now back to Jim and Greg, participated heavily in the performing arts. They appeared together in plays as well as wrote and performed skits for the school's Variety Show affectionately called "The V-Show." In one skit called "Mathletes" Jim played the coach and Greg his star Mathlete (nerdified with glasses and floods). When asked how long he'd been a Mathlete, Greg's character replied, "Since my freshman year." "And how long ago was that?" Puzzled, the star Mathlete gave it his best shot, but ended up pulling out a calculator to calculate the answer.

Out of high school, the duo spent a ridiculously short time studying film at Columbia College in Chicago where they continued to shoot short films as well. In one Jim was delivering packages and slipped on a banana peel. Perhaps not the height of sophistication, but it drew laughs from later viewers. In another, set in a real grade school classroom, the bit required Greg to play a grade school student, sitting amongst actual students of a class that was taught by Jim's sister Gayle. There was also a short called "Clipped Toenails," where Greg ran around looking for some place to throw the nails he'd just clipped because everywhere he went there was a sign telling him that clipped toenails were prohibited. Greg liked putting regular characters doing regular things in uncomfortable situations, finding the humor building as both the inconvenience and the discomfort grew. A lot of comedic power could be found in those small situations.

Despite their enthusiasm for moviemaking, the pair had a hard time taking the classes at Columbia as seriously as other students. Once in class, the teacher was talking about hidden symbolism and illustrated this with some film clips. "Our classmates were pointing out some, to us, ridiculous examples of so-called symbolism," Greg remembers. "Jim said to me, 'Watch this,' and raised his hand. 'You see those shadows on the main character? They look like prison bars showing how trapped the character is.' Then he went into a convoluted explanation of the psychology of the scene. Everyone congratulated him on his observation as if it were a sincere take on the art of symbolism in the scene when all it was, was Jim blowing smoke."

Those of a more improvisational nature sometimes lack the patience for the structured environment of a class. For his part, Greg always found hands-on experience the best teacher. The only thing of value he felt he learned at Columbia happened after he got his hands on cameras and editing equipment. In the 1980s, editing a film could be a laborious process involving cutting the physical film that had been shot and splicing it back together with actual tape, while reels of film ready for editing hung all over the room. "Back then we used a Bolex camera and 16 mm black and white film," he explained. A Bolex camera, produced by the Swiss company the Paillard Company, weighing around 6-8 pounds, was not a huge piece of tech considering the result. Certainly, the late 80s would see video cameras that were much more cumbersome in size and portability. But compared to what is available now, in both home and professional moviemaking, it was a substantial piece of equipment. "I don't think any film school uses actual film these days," Greg added.

Eventually, Greg and Jim left Columbia, turning their focus to the Second City. Or at least The Players Workshop at Second City. Started in 1971 by Josephine Forsberg, the workshop's notable alumni include Bill Murray, Shelly Long, Tim Kazurinsky, Harold Ramis, Bonnie Hunt, and George Wendt. Players was unique in that, at the time, it was the only school of improvisation in the country, participants expected to take a 12-month course that had a syllabus before they could graduate. It offered a comfortable place for people from all walks of life to engage in the art of improvisation and gain a better understanding of stagecraft and the elements of live performance. While the workshop wasn't affiliated with the fabled comedy institution, those who desired to pursue a career in comedy often hoped they could move on to joining the Second City stage once they had graduated from the course. Josephine Forsberg also produced shows for the Children's Theater of the Second City, which allowed many of her Player's Workshop students to join those casts.

Classes were intense, creative, and energetic, with students expected to observe and participate in original work performed on the stage.

It was one of these sessions that implanted the germ for what would become *Meet the Parents*. Jim played the father of a girl that Greg was dating. The details of the sketch are vague, but the thrust of the comedy seemed to lie in the father's hostility to his daughter's innocuous paramour. At the end of the workshop, a graduation show was put on using some of the best skits from past exercises. Greg and Jim's *Meet the Parents*-type sketch didn't make the cut, but Greg filed the idea away anyway, sure that something might come of it down the line.

After The Players Workshop, Greg and Jim tried to carve out a place for themselves in the world of showbiz, but it was hardly a smooth path. Jim went on acting auditions, but, understandably, there wasn't much call for a 19-year-old character actor.

To make ends meet, Greg found himself working in the Scharringhausen Pharmacy in uptown Park Ridge but left the job after they wouldn't let him off for work to be an extra in the film *Risky Business*.

The duo even tried to revive their old comedy team, and with the chutzpa of youth, approached the manager of a Ground Round Restaurant in Des Plaines for an audition. Ground Rounds served American fare in a casual, even permissive atmosphere (people were encouraged to throw their peanut shells on the floor) where, depending on the restaurant, a little theater might be mixed in. They were well known for their kids' parties as well as screening cartoons and silent movies on a screen in the restaurant. Right up Greg and Jim's alley.

Renamed Two for the Price of One, the duo performed a free set in the corner of the restaurant during their inaugural tryout. After a few sketches, Jim tried out his new idea called "the informal comedian", an improv-type bit where he would talk to the audience. The act was a hit, thanks in part to the large table of young guys dining there that night who could completely appreciate the humor of the young comics. Greg remembers. "We thought we'd hit the big time! There were so many Ground Rounds and similar restaurants that we could book ourselves at any number and we'd be performing every night." The night they were officially scheduled to perform, however, turned out to be a disaster. This time, rather than college students, the restaurant was packed with families trying to enjoy their meals, uninterested in the two guys talking loudly in the corner. Chagrined, they slunk off to a booth and just stared at each other. The thought of doing a second show was too much to contemplate so they packed up their props and what remained of their self-confidence and snuck out, too embarrassed to go ask the manager for their money. Two for the price of none!

A Standup Guy

By the time Two for the Price of One had given up their dreams of making the Ground Round circuit, Greg had already dipped a toe into the world of standup comedy. The previous summer, Jim had discovered The Comedy Cottage, a comedy club in the neighboring village of Rosemont. Standup comedy had reached its zenith during the 1980s, and it seemed as though a new comedy club was opening every other week across the U.S. Most were highly successful. Bars, restaurants, and dance clubs suffering from the demise of Disco all tried pulling people in with comedy, and the audiences came in droves.

The Comedy Cottage itself was a former disco, converted into a comedy club in 1975 when comedian Tom Dreesen approached owner Ed Hellenbrand and encouraged him to offer comedy on Monday nights. Dreesen himself was no slouch when it came to comedy, having teamed up with Tim Reid in the late 60s to create the country's first biracial standup comedy team. Once the team broke up, Dreesen became a gig comic, eventually taking on the role of regular opener for Frank Sinatra. The popularity of stand-up would help make big-name stars out of people like Jerry Seinfeld, Whoopi Goldberg, and Eddie Murphy, as well as already-established comedians like Robin Williams and George Carlin. Recognizing a good thing when he saw one, Ed Hellenbrand decided the time was right to convert his Maroon Racoon Disco into a Comedy Cottage.

While Two for the Price of One was no more, both comics hit the stage at the Comedy Cottage, though they performed separately. "I had been very active in theater in high school and only agreed to give it a try because I remembered Don Martello, my drama teacher, telling me I had the best comedy timing of any student he had." The beloved drama teacher's words ran through Greg's mind when Jim suggested they perform at open mic night in September of 1982.

As with their audition at The Ground Round, a bit of luck played into the first appearances at the Comedy Cottage since they took place on the Sunday before Labor Day and the place was packed. Greg chose a bit that was admittedly a slight rip-off of the famous "Chuckles the Clown" scene from *The Mary Tyler Moore Show*. In Greg's version, he played an earnest eulogizer who, no matter how hard he tried, couldn't control his laughter over the ridiculous way the dearly departed had departed this life. Thanks to the packed room, both their sets were very successful. Unfortunately, the following week, with a much smaller audience, they both bombed.

While Jim Vincent eventually gave up being a comedian, Greg continued attending the open mics, honing his comedic skills and developing material that worked well for him. It was a slow process, and a long time passed before he was hired by Jay Berk, the general manager of the club, though Greg had a feeling that it was not so much for his comedic skills as much as he happened to be standing by the other guy Jay was hiring. "I guess you're ready too," was the owner's comment.

"Everyone who wants to do comedy needs a club like the Comedy Cottage," Greg stated. "I believe the audience tells you what kind of comedian you should be. Put 50 or 60 people together and they're brilliant judges when it comes comedy (not so much when it comes to politics)."

On first hire, a comedian at the Cottage only had to do a five-minute set. Dumping the derivative eulogy bit, Greg started to talk directly to the audience. Inherently shy by nature, being natural while talking to a crowd of people didn't come easily at first. The secret, he soon discovered, was to treat the audience like they're a group of your friends. Much of his material was taken from funny little things he stated offstage to friends who acted in essence like barometers. If they laughed, he tried using the material on stage.

Back in the mid-80s, the top pay at the Cottage was about $7.50 for a ten-minute set. Many famous comedians had either started at the club or worked it early in their careers. Comedians like Judy Tenuta, Arsenio Hall, and Emo Philips were early discoveries of Hellenbrand.

Greg's signature at the time was a five-minute bit where he did every episode of the old TV show *Kung Fu*. He performed all the voices and even the theme song and it remained a popular bit for ten years until it out-aged the audiences who hadn't seen the show.

There were other clubs around, like the Comedy Womb in Lyons, and Who's on First in Elmhurst, not to mention the many downtown Chicago venues. After six or seven months, Greg had developed a good half hour of material that worked consistently. Soon he began receiving calls from club owners looking to book him. "I never sent out a press kit or contacted a club to get booked," he said. "It all just happened. I rode the wave and soon was a full-time, professional comedian."

It was fellow comedian Chaz Elster who introduced him to his first out-of-state gig when he asked Greg to open for him in Lansing, Michigan. A man by the name of John Yoder booked Michigan, and parts of Ohio and Indiana. Greg usually had a regular comedy club, which the comedian would play on the weekend, then he would find "one-nighter" gigs for Tuesday and Wednesday, usually at a restaurant or disco. He remembers killing in the comedy clubs but found performing for a week-night audience from behind a salad bar at some local eatery a bit more challenging. "I've done shows in bars, bowling alleys, basements and the worst were outdoor shows. In the daytime. Comedy is definitely a night thing."

It was those years "in the trenches" doing shows, night after night that gave Greg a real education to what audiences laughed at. "It could be a room full of drunks or a room full of elderly people. I did the same act in Bloomington as in Winnipeg and they laughed at the same stuff in the same spots. I later noticed that with films."

By 1985, Greg was working as the opening act for big stars in big theaters. Opening for the magician, David Copperfield, before an audience of 4,000, when the show started, and the announcer greeted, "Welcome to the magic of David Copperfield!" the cheer that followed would grow silent after he followed with, "But first, please enjoy the comedy of Greg Glienna."

"You could hear, at least in my mind, a sigh of disappointment. But at least those audiences were seated in an auditorium and paying attention." That wasn't always a given when playing comedy clubs where waitresses flew by taking drink orders and small groups of people chatted about any topic that struck their fancy while hecklers weren't shy about making their presence known. Greg wasn't allowed to hang around after his sets during the Copperfield run and was escorted out after his performances. "I guess they were afraid I'd steal his magic tricks or something."

Opening for crooner Bobby Vinton proved to be a little difficult. "He attracted a mostly older crowd, many of whom were bussed in from nursing homes. Here I was, this 21-or-22-year-old kid wracking my brain for ideas that would appeal to old people. To make matters worse, one of his songs was a *Phantom of the Opera* medley and he had smoke machines on stage behind me which would emit a puff every few minutes. I'd be trying to find anything that an older crowd could relate to, then it would 'puff' behind me, scaring the audience. 'Young man, young man, fire!' a chorus of voices would shout out. I'd turn and see nothing and go on with my act. 'Fire! Young man!' Eventually, I said, 'If there's going to be a fire, let me finish so I can get out of here safely!'"

Opening for Connie Francis gave Greg the chance to invite his parents to the concert and his mom, a fan of the singer since she was young, was able to hear her idol sing live.

He also opened for actor/singer Jack Waggoner who was a teen idol at the time thanks to his role as Frisco Jones on the TV soap opera *General Hospital.* The audience was made up of young women and girls and the entire theater was buzzed by their excitement and heady with perfume. "I guess they liked me," Greg said, "because they would scream when they liked a joke and after I finished. It was a blast, and I got a glimpse of what it must be like to be a teen idol."

Life as a traveling standup comic brought Greg into contact with future stars such as Bob Odenkirk who would later earn fame with shows like *Mr. Show*, *Breaking Bad*, and *Better Call Saul*. (Interestingly, Odenkirk would be one of the stars of the ensemble show *The Ben Stiller Show*, led by the man who would end up portraying the lead in the 2000 remake of *Meet the Parents*). Greg himself would use Odenkirk in his first big-budget feature film, *Relative Strangers*, but that was still in the future. Greg found Odenkirk hilarious but didn't feel the man's heart was in standup. According to Greg, Odenkirk was determined to be a writer for *Saturday Night Live*. He remembered one time seeing the future actor in the green room between shows at the club Who's On First, writing a sketch he'd hoped to send to *SNL* about Sherlock Holmes and his drug use. "He was fearless with his standup material." One night, when they were hanging out at a club between performances, Greg commented that a comic could make a good living at the time doing nothing but talking about the TV show *The Brady Bunch*, since it seemed thousands of comics were doing *Brady Bunch*-bits. The two improvised a bit which they started naming actual episodes. "Hey, remember the one where the family went to Hawaii?" and, "Remember the one where Marsha gets hit with a football and her nose is messed up" which soon became, "Remember when the boys got locked in a meat freezer? And they found their frozen bodies the next day? And there was jizz frozen mid-stream in the air?"

"Well, Odenkirk went up during the next show and performed that bit!" Greg remembered. "Of course, the audience responded when he brought up the real episodes but when he started embellishing with fake plots there was silence—except for me laughing in the back. That's what I mean. Fearless!"

Comedian Jeff Garlin (*Curb Your Enthusiasm*) proved to be another fearless performer. Garlin made doing gigs from hell much easier because he just didn't care and would get up on stage and tell the audience how stupid they were. Once, while bombing at the Comedy Womb, Garlin finally told the crowd that as rubes, they were unable to comprehend the brilliance he was offering them. "I know what you want," he told them. "You just want to hear impressions of Floyd the barber from *The Andy Griffith Show*!" He then proceeded to do a commendable impression of Floyd…if Floyd were in the throes of an orgasm, writhing on stage for at least 10 minutes. "Oh, Andy…ooh Opie's a good boy!"

The quieter the audience got, the harder the comedians in the back of the room laughed, and the longer Garlin felt compelled to sell the bit, playing now more for his fellow comics than for the audience.

Greg also worked with Tim Allen right before his career blew up with the TV show *Home Improvement* and the young comedian could tell right away that this was a guy to watch. Always dressed in a suit, Allen performed with an air of authority and the audiences loved him. Allen requested that Greg be his opening act in Fort Wayne, Indiana at a club named Snickerz. Club owner Kevin Ferguson also used the club as a location for his local TV show *Night Shift*, which featured stand-up, skits, and off-the-cuff comedy. Greg would perform on the TV show on Tuesday, and then work at the comedy club the rest of the week. The TV show also gave Greg a chance to show the short movies he'd begun filming leading Tim Allen to refer to him as "The Albert Brooks of *Nightshift*" (a reference to filmmaker Albert Brooks making six shorts for *Saturday Night Live*'s debut season in 1975).

"Tim and I got along great," Greg stated. "We had dinner several times and hung out after the show. He told me that he had served time in prison for drugs before he became a comedian. A few years later I was in a supermarket, and I saw him in the headline of one of those tabloid magazines. The headline was about Tim's shocking prison past, and I thought to myself, 'Wow, he's really a star now! He's in the tabloids!'"

Enter the Shorts

A comedy show typically consisted of an opener/emcee, who opened the show for about 10 minutes to warm up the audience; then a middle act who typically did about 20 or 25; then the headliner, who would do about 45 minutes, maybe an encore. Not interested in headlining, Greg made enough money as the middle act to afford the studio apartment he had moved into once his parents divorced and sold the family house. While he would remain a full-time comedian throughout the 80s and 90s, Greg began to realize that, like Bob Odenkirk, his heart wasn't in stand-up either. He enjoyed the chance to travel and stay in hotels, but the stand-up club scene began drying up in the 90s thanks in part to its availability on cable TV stations like HBO which meant audiences could enjoy the jokes from the comfort of their own home.

The fact was, Greg Glienna still wanted to be a filmmaker. Whenever he could save up the money and fit it into his schedule, Greg made short films, the sort he ended up showing on *The Night Shift* in Fort Wayne.

As Greg remembered it, "I knew a guy named Mike Cattalico and he owned his own 16 mm camera. His wife Chris had a Nagra tape machine which was a standard audio recorder for movies and TV at the time, and she would do sound when required. Mike charged me $100 for his services and the use of his camera. The footage would then be transferred to ¾ inch video, which gave the shorts a 'film' look. At that time, and even today, to some people, film looked superior to video, but I still had the convenience of editing on video. I could rent an editing deck at the Cable Access Studio in Skokie for a reasonable rate, though I didn't always need sound because I was so enamored with silent comedy that many of my shorts were silent save for the incidental music."

As a kid, Greg would rent black and white, silent films from the Park Ridge Library. Charlie Chaplin, Buster Keaton, and Laurel and Hardy most of all. In many of the shorts Greg would later make, one could see how Keaton's stoic, deadpan performance inspired his own. The style has a purity that lowers the risk of the comedian's reactions, upstaging the humor of the situation. What really woke his passion for silent comedy was seeing a double feature of Chaplin's classic *Modern Times*, and *City Lights* at the Varsity Theater in Evanston. "If you see a silent comedy the way they were intended to be seen, on a big screen with music and an audience, they play like they probably did in the 1920s with the same energy in the audience. Buster Keaton's *The Cameraman*, Harold Lloyd's *The Kid Brother*, and films by a comic called Harry Langdon, were a few of my favorites."

Living in Park Ridge, in the days before the Internet and You-Tube, the height of success when it came to making a short film was to have it presented on a TV show called *Image Union*. Produced by Tom Weinberg, *Image Union* began its run in 1978 and was broadcast on WTTW, Chicago's Public Television station. The program offered independent filmmakers an outlet to show their work at a time when few outlets were available. Rounding up his old film-making partner Jim Vincent to act as producer, Greg began work on a short film titled "Wake Up," based on a standup bit, he did about how hard it was to get out of bed in the morning. Starting with a dream sequence where a beautiful girl is calling to him, the sound of her voice suddenly turns into an alarm clock and Greg awakens, realizing he was dreaming. The rest of the film becomes a monologue as Greg remains in bed trying to convince himself to wake up.

Image Union accepted the film, paying Greg and Jim a few hundred dollars for the chance to show it. With a new calling, Greg acquired a new routine: He worked out of town one or two weeks a month, and the rest of the time played local clubs and made short films. The next short film, actually two shorts filmed the same day, was called "The Exterminators" starring Greg and Scott Bussert, a friend from high school. Arriving on the scene in a white van on which was emblazoned the words "The Exterminators" on the sides and wearing white jump suits, they hopped out in search of some unsuspecting, obnoxious soul to put in his place. Once a perpetrator was found, they looked at each other in silent agreement, then got some dynamite from the van and very matter-of-factly handed it to the obnoxious person. In one short it was a car salesman. The second one was a mime. As the confused perpetrator studied the dynamite, the Exterminators went back into the van, and well… exterminated: pushing down a plunger and blowing the person up. Each of the two films ran under five minutes.

The role of the car salesman was played by a friend of Greg's and a fellow stand-up named Vince Maranto. Maranto would appear in several more films over the years including the original *Meet the Parents*. The part of the mime was supposed to be played by an actor he knew from the improv scene named David Pasquesi, who went on to do small parts in several films directed by Harold Ramis. Pasquesi had agreed to do the film, telling Greg he had the perfect outfit, a striped shirt, and a beret. When they arrived at the Lincoln Park filming location though, Pasquesi was nowhere to be found. Phone calls went unanswered. Deciding to drive to his home, they found Pasquesi just as he was leaving, the surprised look on his face when he saw them indicating that he had forgotten about his date with short film destiny. In fact, he stated that he was just on his way to an out-of-town gig. Annoyed, Greg never-the-less needed the shirt and beret and asked Pasquesi if they could at least borrow them.

Crewmember Alan Martin was drafted to play the part of Obnoxious Mime and was able to pull it off. While *Image Union* wasn't interested in the short featuring the car salesman, they did buy the one featuring the mime.

The case of the missing mime illustrates the occupational problems inherent in independent film making when the production team can't afford to pay people top dollar...or anything, for that matter. It would not be the first time this financial reality would plague a Greg Glienna production.

The Vase

If the original *Meet the Parents* spawned the Universal remake, then the seeds for both could be found in a sketch that Greg and Jim performed at the Players Workshop years before where Jim played the disapproving father of a girl Greg was dating. Greg had reached back into his mental filing cabinet to find that sketch and decided to streamline the concept for the short film "The Vase." The plot was simple. Boyfriend meets girlfriend's parents for the first time. Smiling parents, seemingly accepting of their daughter's choice, ask if boyfriend would like the honor of viewing their prized vase that was kept on a pedestal in a sacredly lit part of the house. When offered the chance to get closer to the vase, boyfriend accepts, staring at it reverently, trying to ignore the oddness of the family's obsession with the vase. Then turning to expound on the rest of the house, boyfriend waves his arms and inadvertently knocks the exalted vase from the pedestal. The sound of glass breaking is followed by Mom's horrified screaming before the scene fades to black. As the next scene begins a clock is heard ticking in the background. Boyfriend looks up and notices Mom weeping. Dad glares at him with undisguised hatred. Then boyfriend notices hanging on the wall a framed portrait of the honored vase.

Filmed as a silent film in black and white, music and sound effects were used to set the mood, and dialogue was presented using title cards. Jim was too young to play the part of the father, so a local actor named Walt Swik was taken on for the role. Jim and Greg appeared with Swik in *You Can't Take It with You* with the Park Ridge Community Players. Greg played the boyfriend. Greg's Aunt Pat Glienna played Mom while the girlfriend was played by someone who had taken the Players Workshop class with Jim and Greg named Nancy Clark.

While at heart the film's plot was similar to the plot of the sketch from the Players Workshop, the tone had been changed slightly. The parents did not start out disliking the boyfriend as the father did in the sketch. Quite the contrary. They were cordial to the young man their daughter was interested in. Even invited him to view an object near and dear to them. For Greg's part, he was perfectly polite, and on his best behavior. But for one innocent mishap, all would have been well. Since it was a short film, the idea was unable to be developed beyond the loss of a very beloved vase. But at that core is the inspiration for the original *Meet the Parents*. A nice guy goes to meet his nice girlfriend's nice family and through a series of freak mishaps, they grow to despise him.

After "The Vase" was shot the folks at *Image Union* bought it which meant it aired to an audience of several million people in the Chicago area. One of those people would later play a larger part in the *Meet the Parents* story.

Greg's next short, which would also inspire a later movie, had its beginnings too on the stage of the Players Workshop. "The Manures" featured the characters of Frank and Agnes Manure delivering a housewarming gift to their new neighbors but spending a good portion of the visit arguing amongst each other as the young couple looked on uncomfortably. After the couple manages to get the Manures out of their house, the husband turns to his wife and declares, "We're moving!"

The actors playing the young couple in the sketch could do little more than set up the scene before being drowned out by the adlibbed vitriol being thrown between the actors playing the Manures. Realizing that the short would need to be a little more structured, Greg wrote actual lines for the characters though, at some point, the Manures were allowed to argue with each other unscripted for several minutes. (Years later, when the characters were used in his film *Relative Strangers*, Greg tried to get Danny Devito and Kathy Bates who played the Menures to do the adlibbed arguing, but they didn't feel comfortable with adlibbing, and he ended up having to write out the dialogue of the argument).

The short was filmed at the home of Greg's sister Victoria and her husband Tim. Comic Vince Maranto again joined the production playing the male half of the young couple while the female was played by Mary Ruth Clark, a name that would figure prominently in the *Meet the Parents* story. Mary Ruth was recommended by a guy named Peter Burns who Greg knew from the improv scene in Chicago. Burns and Clarke were both a part of a well-regarded theater troupe called the Friends of the Zoo and according to Burns, Mary Ruth was someone with a great scream. Greg met her at her place in Lincoln Park and the two creatives hit it off. The part didn't call for any screaming, just crying, but Mary Ruth turned out to be perfect for the role. As for Pete Burns, he was honored later when script writers Greg and Mary Ruth used his last name as the surname for the parents in the original *Meet the Parents*.

The strength of this short featuring the Manures is that it was shot as a horror film, using all the standard horror movie cliches: ominous music, shadowy lighting, and low angles. It was called, "The Housewarming" and to keep the film under budget, props were often homemade. For example, The Manures welcome the young couple to the neighborhood with a massive cheeseball about the size of a basketball. A cheeseball that size would have probably cost about $100 if real cheese had been used, so Greg instead covered a big balloon with papier-mâché, then spread processed cheese and nuts over it producing for his efforts a remarkably realistic-looking fake cheeseball.

As with all his shorts, they filmed it in one day, going late into the night, much to his sister's annoyance. The effort was worth it though. Not only did *Image Union* run it during their regular show, the show's producers also included it in their New Year's Eve special, which meant it aired twice, and Greg almost broke even with that one. He even got a fan letter for it.

The film-making bug had bitten him and bitten him hard, and Greg was now more certain than ever that his future lay in the movies.

Used car Prices

In 1988, the book *Feature Filmmaking at Used-Car Prices* was published and hit the young filmmaker population like a bombshell. In it, author Rick Schmidt laid out how to "Write, Direct, Shoot, Edit and Produce a Digital Video Feature for Less than $3,000." Which of course, even back then, was unheard of.

"It changed my life," Greg said. "I was never actually able to make a film for that low, but the book did start me thinking about how I could shoot a feature film." (It's interesting to note: the book's second edition published in 2000 raised the budget dramatically to $15,000).

Following the book's advice could prove risky, however, as Greg discovered when two would-be directors that he knew used their credit cards to finance production and it did not fare well. One of Greg's friends from school, under the spell of Schmidt's book, used his credit card to make a horror film practically unwatchable. "It was so bad it was hilarious. Along the lines of Tommy Wiseau's *The Room*." Having already spent $10,000, the guy was ready to throw more money at the production, hoping to fix scenes he was sure would raise the quality of the film. Greg suggested he throw on a music track and hope he could peddle it as a comedy. Not exactly what the budding filmmaker wanted to hear, hence the friendship ended.

Of course, the moral to the story is that while a film could be made for a low budget, it still needed to be good if it was going to be successful. Greg's efforts in making short films helped him understand the logistics of filming. By the 1990s, the home video market had opened up and there stood a good chance, if the film was good enough, to make back the initial investment on such a project. The time was right for Greg to try feature filmmaking.

He chose to make a feature out of "The Housewarming," keeping the horror movie tone of the short and calling it *They Came from Next Door*. All he needed was to track down $10,000.

Out of the main clubs he played, Greg had a particular affection for working out of The Funny Firm comedy club. Located on Grand Avenue in Chicago, it had a huge room that could hold 800 people when sold out, which it frequently did. The owner/brain of the business was Len Austrevich, a local comic himself who, along with Nick Hendricks, Mike Promen, and Mike Gauthier, opened the club in December of 1987. They were up against some stiff competition in the comedy market particularly from Zanies which had a club on Wells Street in Chicago as well as a location in the Northwest suburb of Mount Prospect. But according to a *Chicago Tribune* article of Dec. 11, 1987, Austrevich said, "We want to be innovators, try new things. It's time comedy clubs grew up."

To that end, the folks at the Funny Firm looked for innovative ways to get people to their club. They were the first, for example, to pioneer the "giveaway" method of filling a comedy club in which customers were given cards to fill out for the chance to win free tickets. A small army of telemarketers then called the phone numbers on the card to give the people the exciting news that their cards were winners. The thing was, all the cards were winners. The idea was to get the seats filled. Whatever was lost on the cover charge was amply made up for with the two-drink minimum since patrons at a comedy club rarely held themselves to a two-drink minimum.

Some comics blamed Len Austrevich, whose brainchild this was, for helping to bring on the death of the comedy scene as audiences became accustomed to not paying a cover and smaller clubs couldn't survive with just the revenue from drinks. But that would be in the future. In 1988, the club was a huge success and Len was making money hand over fist.

A gambler in more than just business, Len had just won a huge windfall in Las Vegas when Greg approached him with his "used car" pitch to convince him to finance the film he was hoping to make. Len had seen "The Housewarming" short and thinking a feature was a great idea, forked over $10,000 to help it become a reality.

After writing the script, Greg gathered the cast of "The Housewarming" to reprise their roles in *They Came from Next Door*. Along with the original cast, Greg's Aunt Pat was cast as well as several Chicago comics, including Mark Roberts who was a standout in the film. A great comedian and actor, Roberts is now most famous for his writing on the sitcoms *Two and a Half Men* and *Mike and Molly* (the latter of which he also created. In fact, the character of Molly's mother's boyfriend is named after his *They Came from Next Door* co-star Vince Moranto). Roberts played a friendly priest who is finally driven over the edge by The Manures. "He was the first experience I had with an actor really bringing more than I imagined to something I wrote," Greg remembered. "He said sanctimonious lines in a completely flat, deadpan style which hinted at the character's later mental breakdown."

Another impressive cast member was local comic Jeff Schlessinger who played a too-eager realtor anxious to sell the couple the house before The Manures showed up.

They Came from Next Door became Greg's "college education." The budget rose to $15,000 from the original $10,000 he quoted to Len Austrevich and for a feature film, even $15,000 didn't allow for the niceties of multiple takes. "I foolishly decided to make the film, not only a horror parody but a low-budget horror parody. I encouraged the actors to over act, in a campy way, which never works on film." This teachable moment in time taught him that even the broadest of jokes must be played with believability. "My hero Charlie Chaplin said it best. 'If what you're doing is funny, you don't have to be funny doing it.' This served me well with subsequent films but this one was the guinea pig and suffered for it."

Not only was the acting frequently over the top, but Greg purposely shot it in an amateurish way, with long shots and people sitting in chairs saying their lines instead of getting movement in a scene.

Not that there weren't some good points to the film. "There's a charades game in that film which I used verbatim in my film *Relative Strangers*. In *Strangers,* Edward Herman was the guy giving clues, getting more and more annoyed by the inept Menures, who didn't quite understand how Charades is played. In *They Came from Next Door*, Mark Roberts played that scene totally straight, like a ticking time bomb, and made the scene hilarious when he eventually exploded. Edward Herman was a naturally funny guy but he played it too funny in *Strangers*. By that I mean, he was playing it like he was in a comedy. I like comedy played like a drama which lets the writing be funny. I guess I had been spoiled by Mark's performance and one of the problems with directing stars is: You don't get to rehearse. I met Edward, a great guy. The day we filmed the charades scene, we had a big day with a lot of pages to film, so I really couldn't get the performance I was looking for from him. I eventually just had him stare deadpan and I could cut in when needed."

By shooting *They Came from Next Door* in such an amateurish way, by thinking that a parody of a cheesy horror film needed to look cheap, Greg forgot an important element to film making: The audience subconsciously expects everything to be real. In certain cases, they will allow for certain exceptions by suspension of disbelief, like the existence of vampires or a fantasy world, like the *Lord of the Rings* films. But everything else must be believable. Anything that takes the audience out of the story, like bad writing or bad acting, or a microphone coming into view, will annoy them because for 90 minutes or more they want to believe it's actually happening. They are voyeurs.

They say experience is the best teacher and Greg learned a lot from this experience. The film was finished in 10 days and had some screenings, but nothing more really came from it.

Emo

Emo Philips looks a bit like the love child of Charlie Chaplin and Buster Keaton with a soupçon of Clara Bow thrown in for good measure. Given Greg's affection for the silent movie greats, it's little wonder the two hit it off. Born in Chicago and raised in Downers Grove, Illinois, Emo came onto the comedy scene in the mid-70s sporting a New Wave Bohemian look and a neurotic-style stage presence that assisted the punch lines sneaking up on the audience. And while Emo's physical mannerisms made it seem as if he might just as likely rush off the stage in a panic attack before delivering the punch lines, those punch lines he delivered were gems.

"I had quite a laugh today at the expense of the service station attendant who was attempting to scrape the bird droppings off my windshield. I never let on that they were on the inside."

"My girlfriend and I almost didn't have a second date because on the first date I didn't open the car door for her. I just swam to the surface."

Greg met Emo Philips when he was booked to be his opening act in Kalamazoo, Michigan at the Hilton Comedy Club and they remain friends. "I had heard a lot about him from working at the Comedy Cottage where he had played many times when he was starting out. He had graduated from that place by the time I started out."

Emo was such a big attraction that the club in Kalamazoo expanded to three shows a night on the weekend rather than the typical two shows on Friday and Saturday. Greg wound up catching the nasty flu which was unfortunate since if you didn't perform you didn't get paid. Luckily, the club put the comedians up in the hotel that had the comedy club in the basement. It made it much easier for Greg to do his act, take the elevator up to his room, throw up, lie down for as long as he could, then go down and do another show. "I was still able to catch most of Emo's act," Greg stated, "and I was bowled over by his material. Jay Leno once called him the best joke writer in the business, and I agree! Every sentence was comedy gold, and I was somewhat in awe of him."

Feeling better by Sunday's show, Greg planned to drive back to Chicago on Monday and was surprised when Emo asked if he could ride back with him, apparently unfazed by Greg's recent bout of flu. The 147-mile trip from Kalamazoo to Chicago gave the two comedians a chance to discover a shared love for silent comedy and great American comedians like W.C. Fields and Jack Benny. Through the years, the two became good friends, Greg even serving as best man at two of Emo's three weddings. "We've seen and analyzed many hours of classic comedy," Greg said. "Emo said sometimes we were like two Jews discussing the Talmud. Who was the greatest, Chaplin or Keaton? We pretty much agreed that funny as the others were, Chaplin was the greatest overall. He was the only guy who could be funny and break your heart in his films."

As it turned out, Emo had seen "The Vase" on *Image Union* and enjoyed it, though at first, he hadn't made the connection between the young comic and the short film. Once he did, Emo told Greg he'd like to do a short with him and the two exchanged numbers.

In the meantime, Greg made another short he filmed while at the bar at the Comedy Cottage. He played a guy who sat down at a bar only to discover Batman sitting beside him. Not the Michael Keaton Batman of the 1989 movie, but rather the Adam West-version Batman from the 1960s TV show. The idea was that Batman was drowning a broken heart after Robin, the Boy Wonder, ran off with The Catwoman. The part of Batman was played by Greg's friend Mike Toomey, a talented Chicago comedian who has become a bit of a local legend thanks to his creative work on the WGN TV morning news. His Adam West is spot on as is his Caesar Romero version of the Joker. The short was accepted by *Image Union* and

Mike went on to appear in two more of Greg's films including *Meet the Parents*. "Mike has the skill to play many roles and may have been swept up by *Saturday Night Live* or some other show, but with a family in Chicago, he didn't feel like moving to either coast," Greg said.

Shortly after the Batman short was filmed, Emo called Greg with written material for a silent short he called "The Can Man." For a cast, they chose several comics in supporting roles including Bob Rumba and Harry Hickstein (aka Mr. Bigstuff), who looked like a mean biker dude but was a sweetheart in real life. The film was shot around Downers Grove, a village about 22 miles southwest of Chicago, which was where Emo called home between the brief periods he wasn't on the road. The end product turned out to be a 15-minute-long comedy short. After showing it to a test audience though, they cut the film down to seven minutes. Emo was so pleased that he said the short had given him more satisfaction than anything else he had done so far.

These couple of shorts had also gotten Greg's creative juices flowing and soon another idea began to bloom in his mind.

In the 1968 Blake Edwards film *The Party*, the great Peter Sellers plays Hrundi V. Bakshi, an accident-prone Indian actor who is invited to a swanky Hollywood party by mistake and upon arrival, proceeds to innocently destroy the festivities. Bakshi entered the party without ego, perfectly open and friendly, unfortunately on a day when he cannot seem to do anything right. And often what he does goes horribly wrong.

Along with its brilliant sight gags and set pieces, the plot also spoke to Greg. So simple yet with so much comedic potential. Having gotten it into his head to have another go at turning a short film into a feature, he began to think that "The Vase" might just be the one. If *The Party* could just be a guy at a party causing mayhem, why couldn't a film feature a guy who goes to meet his girlfriend's parents and about everything that could go wrong during that does?

"I've always been attracted to ideas that are relatable to a large number of people. The biggest laughs come from things the audience can identify with. Almost everyone has been through the terror of meeting the family of the one you're in love with."

Greg bounced the idea off Jim Vincent who thought it was a winner, telling him that as soon as they had a script, he'd put the crew together. Then Greg decided to see if Emo Philips might be interested in funding the project. Emo had been doing quite well with an HBO comedy special and many TV appearances. "He's a hilarious guy to be around," Greg commented of his friend. "Very different than the way he acts on stage. He will kill me for making this public but offstage Emo is more deadpan and has the quickest mind of anyone I've ever met.

"I've always thought that his distinctive style of performing and the way he uses his body onstage, works against him for a lot of people. As I've said, his material was second to none and could stand up on its own. The exaggerated delivery wasn't needed. I would love to see him go on a show like *Real Time* with Bill Maher, as himself, and give his opinions on world events. He'd make a lot of new fans, in my opinion."

After hearing Greg's vision for the film, Emo agreed that it might make a funny movie, telling him that if he liked the script, he'd consider funding it. Greg could not give him a figure of what it would cost until we saw how long it was and how many locations were required but he assured the potential investor that he'd try to keep the budget down to "used car prices."

Along Came Mary Ruth

Mary Ruth Clark was sitting at a desk in her family's basement study one day, having a phone conversation with her friend, when she happened to notice a news article, she'd seen many times before but never really looked at. "Wow!" she exclaimed, "My dad won a Pulitzer Prize!" In the 1950s, as part of a reporting team covering a bank heist and a siege, reporter John J. Clarke helped win for the Providence, R.I. Journal a Pulitzer Prize for deadline news reporting. "A guy robbed a bank," Mary Ruth explained, "and was on the lam in the neighborhood and my dad was on his trail. He knocked on a door and the guy opened it, and he had a woman in his hands with a gun pointed at her. I didn't know about this until much later."

Mary Ruth Clark inherited a love for the written word from her father as well as his passion for "red penning." "He really excelled at copy editing," she stated. "He was really just a master word-smither. And maybe I inherited that because I'm a red penner. I just red pen everything." But her aspirations were less journalistic, and writing was something she sort of fell into. She was an Equity actor from age 15 to 30 and found herself playing a lot of secondary comic relief characters in musicals. "I got sick and tired of musicals. I only knew the songs I had to sing. Eventually, I found myself migrating to theater companies that were creating their own material." Touring for many years with a company called Wavelength, she found herself in the same company as Bob Odenkirk and Oscar nominee Paul Raci. From there, she joined the company Friends of the Zoo. "I really liked it and sitting around a table with other actors cracking each other up made me realize how much I enjoyed scriptwriting."

After moving to Chicago, somebody told her that this guy Greg needed a screamer for a short film and her name had been volunteered. "We all have our talents." The two met and got along well.

For Greg, the timing couldn't have worked out better. He didn't want to tackle this script alone. There was far too much riding on it. Throughout the two films he had made with her, Greg had become friends with Mary Ruth and realized what a talented writer she was.

"When I told her about the idea for *Meet the Parents*," Greg remembered, "Mary Ruth showed as much enthusiasm for it as she was capable of—I hadn't learned yet that she's not one to tempt fate by having too much hope for anything pleasant ever happening. But she thought it could make a funny film."

They started brainstorming, the two approaching writing from different directions. "Greg's a very intuitive writer," Mary Ruth said of her co-writer. "He's great at capturing an idea that can be universally funny. I'm much more about the structure and character development." The mix worked well. Since there was really no plot, and it didn't have an act one, two, or three like most films, the pair would put each of the disasters, in the series of escalating disasters on 3-by-5 cards and place them in order of their horribleness. And in this film the more horrible, the funnier. Essentially, many walks were taken while they discussed everything that could go wrong meeting the parents.

When writing a scene, since movies are a form of storytelling, Greg imagines a guy in a bar, talking to another guy in the same bar. Would the other guy find what's said interesting? For example, if one guy said, "I heard about a guy once who went to meet his girlfriend's parents and he accidentally put her mother's eye out with a fishing pole" (something that occurs in the film), the other guy would be intrigued. "No shit? Wow! Then what happened?" He might laugh or he might be horrified but he wouldn't be bored.

After the 1992 *Meet the Parents* was made, Greg heard from many people who could commiserate with the hapless character of Greg in the film. "One guy told me that when he first met his girlfriend's family, he went to their house and was told to wait in the living room. He sat down on the couch and heard a cry. It turned out the family cat had a habit of sleeping under the cushions and he sat on it and killed it. I asked the guy what he did, and he said, 'Sat in the chair.' The next day his girlfriend called him in tears telling him the beloved family cat had died. He offered his sympathies, never telling her what had happened."

Greg and Mary Ruth had discussed the boyfriend inadvertently killing the family pet and it was decided that the boyfriend would throw a stick on the water at a lake and the dog would swim out to fetch it and never return. "We thought it would be funny to use the classic shot from Jaws," Greg explained. "In this case, it's the stick, not a girl, floating lonely on the water. We racked our brains thinking of terrible things that could happen on this weekend from hell. A good rule of thumb in any storytelling is: What's the worst thing that can happen? It's human nature to be interested in someone's problems. Gapers' blocks on the highway are termed such for a reason. With comedy, you must have a sense of what's too much. Too horrible and it crosses over to drama or tragedy."

Mary Ruth was pegged to play Fay (named after a voice teacher Greg knew), the crazy sister of Pam, the fiancé whose parents the character Greg (played by Glienna) goes to meet. An idea they had considered but ended up dropping was to make Fay and Pam twins and Mary Ruth could play both parts. This could lead to some predictable mistakes with the character of Greg having a hard time telling them apart. But that came off too gimmicky.

Instead, they decided that Greg's role in the advertising business, having written a commercial that Ed McMahon appeared in, would lead Fay to believe that her sister's boyfriend could be her ticket to fame and fortune as a theatrical singer. Anyone under 50 might not recognize the name, but back in the 80s and early 90s, Ed McMahon was the host of a television show called *Star Search*, which was helping would-be stars achieve their dreams long before *America's Got Talent* or *The Voice* came on the scene. Fay's obsession with the idea that he could introduce her to the powerful host would lead to the character's general harassment of the unsuspecting boyfriend throughout his stay. Their time in cabaret and musical theater left Greg and Mary Ruth with plenty of experience to draw from when it came to the people in that world.

Along with sisters Fay and Pam, the Burns family would consist of typical midwestern parents Dina and Irv. Cheerful, polite, and very open to meeting their daughter's boyfriend.

The tone of the movie would be a horror film, but hopefully one the audiences would laugh at. The tension would build as the escalating mishaps occurred despite the character Greg's best efforts, and it would become a contest to see how much fate could torture the character before he finally blew.

Inspiration came from all over. Mike Toomey, remembering a Victrola from a hotel where the comics stayed in Lansing, suggested it would be funny if the character of Greg turned the handle on the family heirloom and it broke off. Instead of confessing, though, in the film, the character of Greg throws the piece under the sofa.

Jim Vincent once told the story of how he was cutting a roast at the house of his girlfriend's parents and while doing so, it ended up on the floor. A fine addition to the script but as told, the story didn't put nearly enough pressure on Greg. A variation was put on the script in which after the roast comes out of the oven, Greg accidentally spills a glass of wine on it and the table. In attempting to assist his girlfriend in mopping up the mess, he lifts the platter so she can get underneath and the roast slides with excruciating slowness off the platter, onto the floor, where the family dog grabs it and runs off.

Getting caught with a joint, overflowing the toilet, putting the mom's eye out with a fishing pole which was handed to him by the father in the hope of taking him fishing…these were gags designed to escalate Greg's discomfort as the weekend descended into hell.

A lot of time was spent trying to decide upon an ending. The conventional Hollywood way was for everything to be forgiven in the end and to have the parents accept the boyfriend despite the damage caused by him. Being an independent production, the creators had a little more leeway when it came to making the comedy dark. Presenting it as a cautionary tale would allow them to have an unhappy, yet still hopefully funny ending. The film opens with a guy played by Jim Vincent who works at a gas station where he enjoys scaring customers with tales of mayhem and horror. A customer comes in to pay for gas and during the friendly conversation reveals that he's on his way to meet his girlfriend's parents. "Turn around!" the clerk warns, ominously. "I knew a guy once…" Then the rest of the film acts out the clerk's tale about the tragedy that befell another guy who went to meet the parents. After the tale has been "told," action returns to the gas station where the customer, now totally apprehensive about meeting the parents of the girl waiting for him in the car, hurries from the building. Another customer comes in and during the conversation states that he's taking his kids to the circus. The clerk once again stops short and looks at the guy. "Turn around! I once knew a guy…" Fade to black.

One thing Greg insisted upon was that there be no jokes, believing that comedy is much more effective when the situation is funny, but the characters are totally serious. To use another example from his idols Laurel and Hardy, Stan hands Ollie an open can of milk instead of a telephone and Ollie pours it into his ear. Ollie grabs the real phone and says, "Pardon me, my ear is full of milk." A funny line but said sincerely, deadpan. "Emo once sent me a newspaper interview with Don Knotts," Greg said, "who was talking about his days with *The Andy Griffith Show*. In it, Knotts said that Andy would go through the scripts, taking out all the jokes. That's one of the reasons the show is still regarded as a classic."

Greg once had a disagreement with Emo concerning silent films. "I felt and still do that you could take a silent comedy, add naturalistic dialogue, and it would still be funny. The films were funny because of the situations." Once, while on the road with Mike

Toomey, the two comedians went to see a matinee film of *Weekend in Bernie's* and left thinking the film was pretty bad. The only laugh came when the two hapless leads were running to catch a ferry. They make a heroic leap, only to find that the ferry was coming in and that leap hadn't been necessary. "Later I saw that exact same gag in a Buster Keaton silent film. Funny is funny. I wanted *Meet the Parents* to be a silent film that had dialogue." The humor would come from the situations faced with everyday dialogue.

In keeping with the silent comedy tradition, Greg decided to name the main character after himself. "I had noticed that, in their classic films, Harold Lloyd was always Harold in his films. Stan Laurel and Oliver Hardy were always Stan and Ollie. And Buster Keaton was frequently Buster. That's why I played Greg. Not Greg Focker. That came way later. My character never had a last name."

As scriptwriting goes, the writing went quickly and once it was complete and typed up, Greg and Mary Ruth gave a copy to Jim so he could begin budgeting the film.

Remarkably simple compared to now when a script might pass through 50 hands in Hollywood before it finally reaches the filming stage. "Now when I complete a script," Greg opined, "I get notes from my managers, from prospective producers, from actors, and anyone else looking to put in their two cents, and writing the script takes less time than getting it to the draft where everyone is happy with it. Mary Ruth and I just wrote something we thought was funny and put that on the screen."

Of course, to be fair, the stakes are higher with a big-budget Hollywood-type movie put out by a studio employing hundreds if not thousands of people and run by a board of investors expecting a healthy return on their investment. That is where the freedom of an independent lies. The creators are not held to those kinds of constraints so, while of course, it would be great, they don't have to concern themselves with appealing to a general, box-office swelling audience.

At one moment, while Mary Ruth was typing the script out, she remarked, "You know, this isn't exactly a work of art." This started Greg questioning if any of it was funny because while he may not have the pressures of a big studio, this was none-the-less a project close to his heart that he hoped would bring success he could build upon. As it turns out, Mary Ruth had told the idea to an old boyfriend and he told her it wasn't funny, putting the devil of doubt into the process. "That's how fragile artists' egos are and why, to this day, I never tell people I'm around what I'm working on unless I really know they are trustworthy," Greg said. "In fact, I remember being at a party and someone asked about the film I was writing. I said it was about a guy who went to meet his girlfriend's parents, and everything went wrong. He just stared back at me blankly. You have to be careful. Creativity comes from enthusiasm and if you lose enthusiasm, it can dry up."

After reviewing the script, Jim figured the movie could be made for $30,000 with two weeks of shooting. Greg was still shooting for $10,000. With the production set to begin, all that was left was to get Emo's seal of approval on the script. He was relieved when the comedian announced that he liked it, however, Emo admitted that while he liked it, he missed a lot of the big laughs. For instance, later in the film, after the character of Greg has broken the afore mentioned Victrola handle and surreptitiously thrown it under the sofa, a father increasingly annoyed by the mishaps of his daughter's boyfriend takes him out fishing in an attempt to bond. On a boat in the middle of the lake, he turns to the character of Greg, asking, "Did you break my Victrola?" Sheepishly, Greg replies, "Yeah. I was turning it and the handle came off." "Where'd you put it?" After a brief pause, Greg tells him, "I threw it under the sofa." Then the dad turns away from him and the two sit there in silence.

Emo told him he didn't see the laugh when he read the script, but in a theater with an audience, this got the longest laugh of any film he had ever seen. "It's true." Greg said, "I left those two characters sitting in uncomfortable silence for 30 seconds after that exchange and the audience laughed the whole time! David Mamet once said nobody in Hollywood knows how to read a script and I think he's right. Unless you can visualize how it will look once it's shot and edited, you can't judge something as delicate as a laugh."

Emo liked the script enough to put money into it. The project was a go. But Greg realized a lot was riding on this film, including his future as a filmmaker. "I looked upon this as a second chance. The comedy scene in the Midwest was already showing signs of drying up. I had to make this one great!"

The Script is Key

Greg is only too happy to scale a soap box when it comes to the topic of scripts. To him, the script is the most important ingredient of a movie. "That and casting are 95 percent of what makes a good movie. The public goes to movies based on who stars in it or who directs it, but maybe they should also, if they like a movie, consider who wrote it. 'I want to see all they're films!'"

Unfortunately, they don't, and that's why writers don't have half the clout or earn as much as actors or directors. In the theater world, the writer is king. In the film industry, far from it. And it's fascinating to see as the credits scrawl on the screen how "A Film By" is followed by the name of the director, not the writer who actually thought up the story and wrote the dialogue. "If it's a writer/director situation, then it should be 'A Film By' but a director getting that credit is like a building designed by Frank Lloyd Wright not being recognized as a Frank Lloyd Wright building but rather a building by the name of the contractor who supervised the construction."

To Greg's way of thinking, a director gets kudos that, in many cases, should go, not only to the writer but to the actors, the director of photography (DP), and the editor. A good film could conceivably be made with no director, if you had a great script, well-cast actors, a great cameraman or DP, a top-notch crew, and a great editor. In fact, there have been films that have been saved when they've gone back to the editing booth and been re-edited.

But a movie can't be made without a script. "I know some films use improvisation, but that's another form of writing," Greg stated. "When I'm writing a scene, I frequently imagine I'm on stage doing an improv scene. What would I say? I think all writers should take an improv class to hone their skills."

As filmed, the original *Meet the Parents* was a dark comedy, which can be tricky to pull off. Many of the things that happened could be viewed as a tragedy but it's all how it's handled. For instance, frustrated by her inability to get her singing career going (and angry at Greg for not making her *Star Search* dream happen), Pam's sister Fay ends up hanging herself. Around her neck is a sign that says, "Greg killed me!" This usually got a laugh, and no one complained about the film making a mockery of death or suicide. But that's because the sign pushes it over the top, into the area of farce, and the way the film is written, with all the mishaps taking place prior, the audiences' sympathies are with Greg, the protagonist. "I've had people come up to me after screenings and say, 'I felt so sorry for your character.' No one that I heard from felt sympathy for the sister who hung herself. We could have written it to make the audience care about the sister but then that would have been a Tennessee Williams drama."

Same with the family dog dying. "The philosopher Henry Bergson famously said that comedy is a momentary anesthesia of the heart.' Things we might not be able to laugh at in real life, properly presented in a story, we can laugh at. As long as we don't feel too much." It's as old as the joke of a guy slipping on a banana peel. There is nothing funny about the injury, but the shock of it allows us to laugh provided we don't think too deeply about that injury.

"I think that's why comedies don't tend to win prizes like more serious works do," Greg mused. "As Woody Allen put it, 'When you make comedies, you sit at the kids' table.' I think because comedies don't involve as much of our feelings as drama, it's seen as being not as important. They really should have the Best Comedy award at the Oscars. Because the funniest film in the world doesn't have a chance against a drama about the Holocaust."

Many elements go into a successful movie, however, and one element they would need to consider was music, both incidental and pieces specific to portions of the movie.

Before the script was even finished, Greg and Mary Ruth knew they wanted to make Pam's sister Fay a frustrated amateur singer, so a song was needed for her to use with which to torture the character of Greg by forcing him to listen to it. Greg had been writing songs and playing piano since high school. He came from a musical family; his mother had been a singer in her youth and his elder brother David was a piano player. "I never wanted to take the time for lessons, but my grandmother got me a *Liberace Big Note Songbook*, so I taught myself to play." Before the script was finished, Greg finished a song for Fay, but when he played it for Mary Ruth, who would be the one singing it, she thought he was trying to kill her. It's an aria, a parody of theater songs. Part Kurt Weill's "Surabaya Johnny" and several Steven Sondheim theater songs. For the last note, Mary Ruth would need to swoop up two octaves. "She asked me if she should sing it badly," Greg said, "but I told her to do it as well as she could. Mary Ruth is a fine singer with a background in musicals. If Fay were a terrible singer, I didn't think it would be as believable that she thought she could become a star."

In the film, Fay explains that the song was written by her voice teacher, David, with whom she took voice lessons twice a week. "He wanted me to take a lesson three times a week, but Daddy couldn't afford it." The joke is inspired by a real-life friend of Greg's whose mother was taking lessons twice a week. Even though she was not a good singer, her voice teacher wanted her to take one more. A good way to pad the bill.

In the film, when Greg has decided he has to get out of there for everyone's sake, his car mysteriously won't start because, unbeknownst to him, Fay has sabotaged it hoping to strand him there, giving her the chance to sing for him alone in her bedroom. She then bursts into the song, "When Phillip's There" complete with piano accompaniment (played by Greg) on tape.

The fact that Emo's real last name is "Philips" is not a coincidence.

"When Phillip's there,
The world isn't colder when Phillip's there.
When Phillip's there,
I'm not growing older when Phillip's there.
When Phillip's there. When Philip's there. When Phillip's there.
But Phillip isn't always there. Sometimes he is out at sea.
Sailing away on a fishing boat.
And hunting for some catfish that lurk beneath the waves."

The song devolves into a screed about Phillip's drinking, and violence, and Fay questioning whether to endure the abuse. Her last line, finished on a high, screechy note, pleads, "Is there a bus in town I could take?"

Another Glienna original is heard during a sequence where the character of Greg takes the father's car to pick up something from the store. They envisioned a long sequence complete with every kind of near-miss accident occurring. Fire trucks, detours, crazy drivers.

Unfortunately, such a scene would be more expensive than the production's "used car price" budget could afford so they had to drop most of this and have just a few mishaps. For this sequence, Greg wanted to use a song he liked called "Into Each Life Some Rain Must Fall" performed by the Ink Spots with Ella Fitzgerald, but after making inquiries, he found the cost of using the piece would be prohibitive. So, he decided to write a song that would have the same vibe, titling it, "Keep Smiling."

"Keep smiling through your sorrow.
Keep smiling through your pain.
And one day, just remember, the sun will shine again.
Your troubles will be leaving.
And you'll be doing fine!
Keep smiling, just keep smiling.
Keep smiling all the time."

Considering singing it himself, Greg eventually decided it might look a little too strange to have the character singing over a scene he was in, and he was embarrassed by how many times his name would appear in the credits, so he asked his friend, singer/actor Walter Tabayoyong, to perform it.

The other song in the film, *Meet the Parents*, which played over the opening credits, was composed by the financial backer, Emo Philips, himself. It was a breezy song with a catchy, 1950s feel cleverly incorporating events that happened in the film. A montage using the funniest photos of parents that people involved with the production could find served as a visual accompaniment for the song.

"Meet the parents, step right up, and don't be shy.
Meet the parents, you're going to be their kind of guy.
Meet the parents, they're gonna flip over you.
Meet the parents, they're gonna love you like I do."

"When you're filming a truck pulls up to the set every day with a fresh delivery of compromise." Those are the words of Woody Allen, a man with million-dollar budgets. On a $30,000 budget like the one *Meet the Parents* had, compromise is practically a co-star. From a writer's standpoint, it can be frustrating because those perfect scenes coming out of the pen may not be logistically filmable. Filming can be inside or outside, whether it's hot or cold, trying to get a take while airplanes are flying by, or people pass by irritated by a disruption in their routine. Police officers want to see your permits, tired actors have meltdowns, or the owners of the house you're renting to film in are anxious to go to sleep while you're still filming. Then there's the budget and how what seemed like a workable one suddenly balloons because of one unexpected happening or another. Filming a movie can be a hard job, where new problems arise constantly, and the crew can sometimes work 14 or 15 hours straight for the sake of a few moments of celluloid.

While some people thrive on those conditions, Greg much preferred the editing process afterward where it all begins to look like a real film. Editing is when the magic shows up and all the hardship of getting the scenes on film can be forgotten.

Before all that could occur though, legal realities came into play. This was not going to be one of Greg's short features he could make on the fly and peddle to *Image Union*. Low budget while it might be, independent for certain, whatever legalities were needed to make a movie needed to be researched and applied. Peggy Glienna, Greg's mom, had taken a course to be a paralegal, which helped when a corporation was formed for the production. (Peggy also proved helpful in the gathering of props for the film). Greg decided to call his production company CEM Productions, the CEM stood for Climb Every Mountain, as in the Rogers and Hammerstein song from "The Sound of Music." "I picked it because it accurately described making a low-budget film," Greg said. "There are constantly unexpected mountains you run across that you have to climb to finish a film."

With a company forming, Greg began to envision the possibilities of filming future movies in Chicago under the CEM banner and his excitement grew.

A business account at a local bank was opened into which the $30,000 Emo invested was placed. The next detail to figure out was the start date for the production. It was already August 1990, so they decided on a September filming date, realizing that they were cutting it close in the hopes of beating October and the nastier weather it brought to Chicago. With several outdoor sequences, including a picnic at a lake, inclement changes in the weather could be problematic. Mary Ruth was just finishing up a production of Shakespeare's *Twelfth Night* as well, which would create a crunch for her.

Auditions were held on Aug. 23. Len Austrevich gave permission to use the stage of the Funny Firm, so a notice was put into a trade publication Audition News, and since this was pre-internet, email, and social media, the producers obtained a Post Office box for actors to send in their headshots through the mail. To save time, agencies in town were also contacted but none seemed interested in a project with so low a budget.

In the meantime, a crew was gathered. The ability to work fast is a skill that is vital to low-budget filming, but of course, a low-budget film did not guarantee a high rate of pay for the crew. Jim was able to find Bradley Sellers, a great camera guy with whom he had worked on a commercial. Sellers had started as an experimental filmmaker, photographing and directing music videos for the Chicago punk/new wave label Wax Trax! Records. His biggest claim to fame was doing some filming on the indie hit *Henry: Portrait of a Serial Killer*. Since then, he's worked on TV shows like *Curb Your Enthusiasm* and *Top Chef*, and documentaries series such as *HBO First Look*, *American Masters*, and *When Sharks Attack*.

Sellers liked the script and agreed on a salary and when Greg explained his idea for the movie to be shot in a way that the story could be told without sound and the audience would still be able to follow the story and laugh, he understood and agreed to help in that approach.

The crew Jim put together included Mary Carlson, who was the Unit Production Manager (UPM) who, according to Greg, "Does all the 'adult' stuff like budgeting, breaking down the script for shooting (particularly hard on a film this low budget). It can be a no-win situation. She was great at it."

And in charge of craft services making sure the cast and crew had food for the duration was a high school friend of Greg and Jim's, Julie Broeckl.

While the weather was growing colder, there was an upside to not filming in Los Angeles. Finding locations on a low budget was a challenge, but outside of Los Angeles, people are often excited about someone making a movie at their location and don't expect a king's ransom in exchange for the privilege. In one scene, the character of Greg goes to a video store to rent a movie for the family to watch. On the advice of the store clerk (a cameo by Emo Philips), Greg rents an Andy Griffith film called *The Country Doctor*. Unfortunately, it is not the Andy Griffith he's thinking of and the wholesome family film he expected to bring home to his possible future in-laws turns out to be a gore-filled slasher film.

Calling around to local video stores, Greg found one in downtown Evanston, Illinois whose owner was so excited to have the scene filmed there and to have comedian Emo Philips involved that he allowed the use of his store for free. According to Greg, "If you tried that in L.A., the owner would charge $3,000 a day. More if it were a larger production."

Logistics

Writing the script with a low budget in mind meant keeping the locations to a minimum and writing as many scenes as possible where background extras weren't needed. Extras cost money. Essentially, the script required: A gas station; a house where most of the scenes take place; a lake where the picnic takes place; a church; a bar; and a parking lot.

There were also a few driving sequences which meant renting a flatbed truck and putting the car upon it so, during filming, it would look like the car was driving when in fact the car itself wasn't moving at all. Also rented was a device that affixed the camera to the hood of the car to film the actors while crouched in the backseat was the sound person with a microphone, hoping to keep the dialogue as audible as possible.

For the Burns' home, a house in Park Ridge was chosen that was owned by Sybil Wijas whose husband had been a good friend of Greg's dad. Sybil lived with her son Johnny who was in his mid-twenties and was mentally disabled, yet she thought it would be fun to shoot a movie in her home. The house was perfect as the setting of the home for Pam's midwestern parents. Sellars liked all the wood features in it and felt the house would look good on film. There was only one problem: Sybil insisted that the crew not use the upstairs. Thankfully this was a minor inconvenience since there weren't that many scenes to be shot upstairs and a friend of Jim's sister had a house that matched the architecture enough for the production to use that second floor. It being a half hour or so away in the village of Palatine was still workable enough to schedule a few days of shooting there.

For the church where Greg is redeemed in the eyes of the Burns family thanks to a well-worded sermon during the church service, the production was able to rent one of the small rooms at the Park Ridge Community Church which had a small altar and pews.

With filming set to begin on Monday, Sept. 17, there was no time to lose to cast the film. The actors read prepared scenes on the stage of the Funny Firm, and Mary Ruth, Jim, and Greg sat at a table taking it all in. The room wasn't exactly swollen with movie hopefuls more experienced actors perhaps scared away by the fact that it was a non-union shoot. Still, eventually, the perfect cast began to form. At one point, while the actors read their lines, Mary Ruth turned to Greg, stating, "Hey, this actually reads funny!"

Jacqueline Cahill was chosen to play Pam, the prospective wife of the character Greg. According to Greg, "She looked great but real and she made me laugh out loud with her reading of the line, 'Once he put a hat on it' which was referring to an urn that held the ashes of the father's late mother."

Carol Whelan, chosen to play Pam's mother, was not as old as the character was supposed to be, sporting flaming red hair cut in a pixie style. But she assured the producers that she had the perfect wig that would make her look old enough. And her readings proved she could play the part. Also cast that day was a funny actor to play the bit part of the stoner kid with no insurance who hits the father's car that Greg has borrowed.

For the role of the father, they read a member of a comedy duo that played The Funny Firm. He was in his fifties, with grey hair, and when he auditioned for the role, he was fantastic, playing the father as a gruff, slightly pissed-off guy. He and Carol Whelan had great chemistry as the parents. Inconveniently, he was a member of the Screen Actors Guild (SAG) and at the time, the guild didn't have a low-budget category the way they do now. While a budget of $10-30,000 was under their radar, he didn't want to go against his union, so the guy passed on the project, leaving the producers wondering if they would ever find anyone else as funny for the part.

Shortly after the auditions, however, comedian Judy Tenuta filmed a pilot for a potential sitcom called *It Could Happen* which she wrote and funded with her own money. Born in Oak Park, Illinois, Tenuta came onto the comedic stage in the late 70s, billing herself as "The Love Goddess" and brandishing her mini accordion which she used to punctuate her comedy. A mix of observational, satirical, and insult, her comedy could also often be brash and outrageous winning her work in TV, movies, writing, and even music.

At the time she and Emo Philips were married, and Greg was giving her a hand with the sitcom she was working on. While at the studio, Emo brought to Greg's attention a tall, bald man who was at the studio to audition for the role of Judy's father in the sitcom but wasn't quite right for the part. Emo though he might be just right for the role of the dad in *Meet the Parents*. In a private room, he met with Emo and Greg and read some lines from the script, and both filmmakers were pleased with the performance. While not as angry as the comedian that Greg had originally hoped to cast, Dick Galloway was naturally funny and believable as a Midwestern, late middle-aged father (which he was in real life). He came off as the sort of guy you'd like to have a beer with and after seeing him Greg realized that Galloway's approach would be funnier in the film. A down to earth, likable guy trying hard to get along with his beloved daughter's choice for a mate, who was pushed to the breaking point, as opposed to a guy who seemed angry from the start.

"In the remake, they went in the direction we had originally considered, with an angry character (played by Robert DeNiro) who seemed to have an issue right from the first meeting," Greg said. "Our approach slowly built up that animosity between Greg and the dad with each new disaster, which I think worked better as a whole."

No one in the cast had much film experience which could prove challenging. Going broad in a film is very easy to do while the sort of subtlety that Greg was looking for could prove a bit more difficult to achieve. To make sure everyone was on the same page, Greg held rehearsals. "I think of filming as opening night to a play, so to speak," Greg said. "So, I like to have rehearsals beforehand." Something not typically done in film. He would get his first taste of the lack of rehearsal when directing his first big-budget film, *Relative Strangers* in 2006. No matter how much he tried, he couldn't cajole the leads, Kathy Bates and Danny DeVito to rehearse. "I think they're used to getting their rehearsals throughout 20 takes, which of course you can't do on a micro-budget as we had on *Meet the Parents*."

Since the scenes were going to be filmed out of order, as most films are, it was important to run through them from beginning to end to get a sense of continuity. Four rehearsals were scheduled and held at the home of Carol Whelan mainly because she didn't like to drive at night. Perhaps for a good reason. One night when Mary Ruth hitched a ride with her, Carol tried to enter the highway via the off-ramp. Carol could be a bit eccentric, according to Greg. "The first rehearsal day we had to cancel because, as she told us, her dog had accidentally run into her eye, and she was injured and couldn't rehearse. I, of course, was concerned about her being okay to film but she assured me she'd be fine. We had our first actual rehearsal the following day and she looked fine. We were surprised to see her dog was the size of a teacup and we wondered how it running into anyone's eye, could cause any harm."

Carol Whelan's collision with her dog was not the only time a facial wound could have risked filming. Greg was living in Rogers Park, at the time one of the dicier neighborhoods near the lake towards DePaul University, a section of town he often referred to as "No Place to Park" or "The Mistake by the Lake." He had been living in Lincoln Park or Lakeview, but he found a great, spacious apartment for a decent price so was willing to look past the sketchiness of the neighborhood. One night, shortly after moving in, he was returning from filming *Meet the Parents* and, as was typical, had to park a good way from his apartment. As he walked, he saw six guys coming towards him, but he tried to act casually since he had no idea what their purpose was. Until he heard one of them shout, "Get him!"

"Now maybe they were having fun," Greg said, "but all I could think about, considering the filming, was 'Nothing can happen to my face!' We were filming out of order and if I'd gotten a black eye or a swollen nose, nothing would match. So, I booked it all the way home. I never had anything like that happen again, but I moved out of there once my lease was up."

Even before the cast had their first read-through, Greg was adamant that, although it was a comedy, it would be a very uncomfortable weekend for all characters concerned. "I told them to forget that it was a comedy and to play it like it was the most serious drama ever filmed." For the most part, that wasn't a problem. Every now and then, someone would read a line "funny" and he would stop and correct them. "I'd much rather work with hungry actors than stars. It's much easier to mold the performance you want with unknown actors, I've found."

After the four rehearsals, everyone seemed to have a handle on their characters and the tone Greg was looking for.

The film turned out to be a sort of "Who's Who" of Chicago stand-up comedians from the 1990s. Mike Toomey, who played Adam West's Batman so expertly in another Greg Glienna's short played the priest, delivering the sermon in such a soothing, Mr. Rogers' cadence that it inspired the family to give Pam's boyfriend a second chance.

There's a scene at a bar where Pam and Greg go to escape the house to talk, and it's filled with Chicago comics like Tony Boswell, Vince Maranto, Ricky Conner, Diane Alimo, and Kay Caman.

Harry Hickstein, who'd been in "The Can Man," played Pam's ex-boyfriend, while John Dacosse, an actor turned comedian, played the gas station customer to whom the story of Pam and Greg is being told at the beginning of the movie.

Producer Jim Vincent earned the part playing the gas station clerk who uses the tale of Pam and Greg to warn the unwitting customer on his way to meet the parents against doing so. The scene gave Jim a slight problem, however. Or rather, his faulty memory did. "Knowing Jim for as long as I had, and having done numerous plays with him, I knew that memorizing dialogue was not his strong suit. I remember when we were in a production of *You Can't Take It with You* by George S. Kaufman and Moss Hart. I was the xylophone playing suiter of one of the daughters and Jim was an FBI agent, I think. He had a line that he never could quite get right. He was supposed to say, 'God is the State. The State is God,' and he found every possible variation on that line. 'State is the God!' 'God is the state is the God.' 'God is the God of the state!'"

All through preproduction and even leading up to the scene, Greg kept reminding him to make sure he knew his lines. Jim assured him that of course, he knew his lines, but when it came time to shoot his close-ups, the lines came out wrong. "I thought you told me you knew your lines!" Greg demanded, to which Jim replied, with complete sincerity, "I know my lines! I just don't know them in the right order!"

Since time and film stock were in short supply, the camera was focused on Jim, but instead of the actors who were doing the scenes with him, Greg stood next to the camera and read Jim's line, then Jim would repeat it. When the actors were cut into the scene, no one was the wiser.

As with most films, there are details beyond filming to be attended to later. Audio, for example.

In the movie, when Greg, Pam, and the parents are watching the video Greg brought home from the video store, the audience sees only the back of the TV that the family is sitting in front of. Audio elements needed to be added to give the actors something to react to (and to illustrate to the audience the reason the characters were having those reactions). The versatile Mike Toomey was enlisted once again to provide his gift of mimicry, imitating Andy Griffith for *The Country Doctor*. His imitation was so spot on that people later came to Greg and asked him if *The Country Doctor* was a real movie starring Andy Griffith.

In another scene, a distracted Greg is channel surfing which required believable audio for the shows he clicked on that became more and more offensive. A comedian friend of Greg's named Poppy Champlin provided a fantastic impression of Dr. Ruth Westheimer, a sex psychologist popular at the time. "So, the man takes his penis…" the character begins, leading to the sound of a man and woman having sex.

"Recording the sex sounds was one of the hardest things I've ever had to do as an actor," Greg commented, regarding the audio work he and Poppy recorded for the scene at a recording studio in Chicago's Lincoln Park neighborhood. "You wouldn't think so but to do that for a solid minute or two is awkward. We both felt embarrassed doing it."

The cast had agreed to wear their own clothes in the film, which saved on the wardrobe budget. The only exceptions were Carol, for whom the producers had to buy from Kmart a couple of conservative outfits befitting the character's age and background; and Mary Ruth, whose character's fashion tastes were a little more eccentric than those of the actress portraying her. Mary Ruth also needed a big dress for her song at the end. A sequined dress was rented from a costume store that fit the bill, though for Greg it wasn't as "big" as he envisioned. To satisfy that vision would have required a designer to create something and the budget would never have supported that.

Two Weeks of Hell

On a pleasant September night, four police squad cars, dispatched after receiving a rcport from a neighbor, rolled up to the Log Cabin Bar on Potter Road in Des Plaines, Illinois where, judging by the crowd of rowdy people congregating in the parking lot, a brawl was brewing. This was news to the folks in the parking lot though who were simply trying to finish a scene in an independent movie being filmed.

"We chose the bar because it has a rustic, small town look," Greg related, "The scene featured Harry Hickstein as Pam's biker, ex-boyfriend challenging my character to a fight. My character, of course, tries to avoid violence but the ex insists we step outside to settle things. This prompts the whole bar to chant 'Fight!' as they follow us out into the parking lot. Shortly after that, the flashing lights showed up. I guess our extras were believable."

Once they were told that there was a film in progress, the police were at least understanding, and thankfully didn't ask for permits. If they had shown up a bit earlier, the flashing lights might have even added something to the scene. A film with a larger budget might have been able to block off the road and inform the neighborhood of the filming. On a small budget, it's a much more fly-by-night operation.

Filming for *Meet the Parents* was scheduled to wrap on Friday, Oct. 5. Nineteen days to film a script was not a long time and meant, as Greg mentioned during rehearsals, that, barring technical problems or a performance just completely off, one take would pretty much be all they could afford to do. Frequently with comedy, however, the first take turns out to be the best anyway.

The production was fortunate, at least for the beginning of the film, to have a talented lighting guy by the name of Pete Biagi. They were unable to afford his normal rate, but he agreed to give them the days he didn't have anything else booked. After seeing the finished movie when it played at a theater in Chicago, he told Greg, "If I had known how good it would turn out, I would have stayed the entire shoot!" The crew was glad to have him while they could.

The dinner sequences were done on the first day. Included in this scene is a bit where Greg's character causes the roast to fall on the floor into the waiting jaws of the beloved family dog, Bingo. The dog was owned by Mary Ruth's boyfriend, Ed Bouchard, who was extremely proud of the fact that the dog was a vegetarian. Greg didn't anticipate too much of a problem with this. What dog would refuse a lovely roast? Helping in the prop department, Greg's mother Peggy made a beautiful roast which it was hoped, once it was on the floor, Bingo would enthusiastically grab it and run off. Unfortunately, Bingo turned out to be a committed vegetarian, sniffing at the beef, licking it a few times, then casually loping off uninterested.

Bingo's lack of commitment turned out to be a fortunate thing for the scene. Later, adding sound effects of a dog enjoying the feast (which was actually Jim eating a piece of bread during postproduction), the camera was kept on the faces of the family, rather than on a dog showing no interest in a roast. The look of shame on Greg's face, and the looks on the faces of the family trying to politely ignore that their meal has just been given to the dog who sounded to be happily enjoying it only adds to the discomfort of the web Greg finds himself in and makes the scene that much funnier.

Dick Galloway's performance was considered particularly impressive. Dick had gotten into acting, appearing in local plays, after retiring from the insurance industry. He would throw in little reactions and bits of business that made the father, Irv, a very memorable role. "There was a line," Greg remembered, "'Who's ready for roast beef?' and Dick would do this big reaction. He'd end up pointing his finger in the air and smiling. It was a little too broad for what I was looking for and I was going to reshoot but Bradley the cameraman whispered to me that we could easily cut it. The rest of Dick's performance was great though. As was Carol's. It was amazing how putting on a grey wig and conservative dresses aged her. It's a shame our film never got a wide release because I'm sure it would have gotten them both a lot of attention."

A lot of preparation had to be done for this film. The plot taking place over three days meant three different outfits for each cast member. Then the filming itself had to be considered. If lights were set for Irv's chair, for instance, they'd have him run through all the lines he said in that chair for the whole film. Continuity required that details be considered whether it be the outfit he was in or even the cigars he may or may not have in his pocket depending on the scene.

The toughest thing to keep track of turned out to be Carol's eyepatch. In the film, the character of Greg is admiring the fishing pole Irv gives him to use when Greg accidentally hits Kay Burns in the eye with it. When she comes back from the hospital, her eye is covered by a white bandage. Every time they filmed a scene Carol was in, it had to be determined if the bandage was on or off, as well as whether she was in the right outfit. And new bandages had to be continuously made because, under the lights, they would lose their stickiness and get sloppy. "By the time we shot the scene where we first see the bandage, it practically covered her entire face and got a huge laugh, especially since she was smiling and saying how it was fine, and no big deal. This was followed by Dick's line, 'They say she probably won't even lose the eye!'"

Sybil Wijas, the lady whose house the production had taken over to film the Burns family scenes, had no idea what she was getting into when she permitted them to use her home. A small army of people invaded her house, moving her furniture around and staying late into the night filming. Every so often, she poked her head down from upstairs and asked if they could keep it down as she was trying to sleep. "Her son Johnny loved us being there, I think," Greg remembered. "Everyone was very friendly to him. He was kind of like the mascot of the crew."

But it was a very bohemian style of filmmaking. One night, while filming the scene where the character Greg is trying to sleep on the couch, Greg the actor was attacked by a mosquito and his battle with the bug was incorporated into the scene. During this, Bradley the cameraman, Chris the sound girl, and Greg, were the only ones awake. Jim and the rest of the crew were all sleeping, bodies strewn around the room while the filming went on.

One scene set on the couch had Mary Ruth's character Fay, dressed in a skimpy nightgown, coming down to the living room couch to see if Greg wanted to smoke a joint with her. Considering how the weekend was already going, this was the last thing the character would want to do, so he tells her no. "Fay asks Greg if he was sure," Greg said, "and in the script I was supposed to say simply, 'No,' but I improvised while filming, responding, 'I've never been more sure of anything in my life.' It got a huge laugh from the crew, so we kept it in."

At one point, Mary Ruth took Greg aside and told him that she thought he wasn't giving enough as an actor. Greg had been playing the character of Greg with a Buster Keatonish deadpan that he hoped would work. "I learned a lot from watching the old *Candid Camera show*. The original 'hidden camera' was shown before shows like *Punked* or other knockoffs. I noticed that when bizarre things happened, people didn't make faces and exhibit big reactions, they usually kept a straight face, in shock and disbelief. That's what I was going for. My dad, after he saw it, asked why I never smiled in the film. I asked him, 'Is there anything in the story that would make my character smile?' and he conceded my point."

By the time they at last wrapped at the Wijas house, it's very likely Sybil Wijas was happy to see them go and would probably think twice before offering her house for such an endeavor again. According to Greg, though, she was very pleased by the result when she was able to see the movie and was proud to have been a part of it all despite the occasional sleepless night.

The most difficult scenes to shoot were those outdoors in Park Ridge. Park Ridge is about ten minutes from O'Hare International Airport and is within a few flight paths. In a scene in which the character of Greg gets into an accident while driving the dad's car, they used the car of Greg's friend Joey Gyondla which had already sustained some damage since they couldn't afford to wreck a car. But this meant that for the pre-accident scenes, they had to shoot around the damage on the car. Every time they attempted to get through the scene, without fail, an airplane would sail overhead, drowning out the sound and forcing them to cut.

Scheduling conflicts could be a challenge as well. An actor had been cast during auditions to play the bit-part of the stoner that causes the accident with the dad's car. The actor cast had been very funny, but when the day they planned to shoot the scene had to be changed, the original actor cast couldn't make it. Under the gun timewise, the scene ended up being shot with Dominic Streddo, the guy helping with the lights, in the role of the stoner. He had some experience acting and did the part well, but it lacked what the original actor brought to it. In post-production, they tried to help the scene by dubbing his voice with that of Mike Toomey.

The accident itself was filmed in reverse, starting with the two cars touching, then backing up. When the film was reversed and sped up, it looked just like the two cars collided.

For the scene of Greg's oh-too-brief redemption in the eyes of the family, the production used the Park Ridge Community Church, nestled in the heart of what is commonly referred to as Uptown Park Ridge. Greg himself had sung in the choir at the church. They were allowed to rent the smaller altar for the day but had to provide a copy of the script to the church for perusal beforehand. Filming on a weekday in the afternoon meant there were fewer people to enlist as extras so those that were willing were arranged in a certain way so that it looked like there were more people in the pews than there were. Mike Toomey as the minister was able to add a bit of his own stuff to the script during the performance.

Then there was…the lake.

September 12, 1990, for most of the crew, is a day that will live in infamy!

The Burns family decides to have a picnic. It's where Irv Burns plans to go fishing in the hopes of bonding with his daughter's boyfriend. The lake chosen for the picnic scenes was up north, about three hours away from the city, though no one connected with the film can seem to recall what town it was in. Despite the outdoor setting, the shoot should have gone smoothly. Everyone arrived mid-morning with a lot of pages to shoot, but it was a perfect day to do so. There was but one problem: The crewmember in charge of making sure the camera battery was charged, hadn't, which meant a three-hour drive to Chicago for a new battery and a three-hour drive back to the lake to film before the sun set. This is why, while he can't remember the name of the lake, that three-hour travel time to it sticks in Greg's mind. "For six hours we just laid around the park where the lake was while someone went for a new battery. And that was long before cell phones so you couldn't check on the ETA of the returning crew member. We did a little rehearsing and tried to be ready, but all we could do was wait."

Perhaps the most annoying thing regarding this particular hiccup was the shot that was missed. "The crewmember arrived around 4 o'clock. Sunset was around 7 o'clock, but we managed to get everything except one shot I really wanted. We filmed the 'Did you break my Victrola' scene with Dick and me in a small boat. We were only a few feet from shore and the only way for the boat to stay still was for a crewmember to go into the water and hold it in place. I really wanted a far shot, with the tiny boat in the middle of the lake that I thought would make it even funnier, but, due to the uncharged battery, we didn't have time to film it. To this day it pains me to watch that scene."

At last, on Oct. 2, production was moved to the final location, the upstairs of a house in Palatine, Illinois. With only five days scheduled at that location, they had a lot of work to complete. One scene Dick Galloway did not enjoy was the scene in which the character of Greg walks into the bathroom and Irv is sitting on the toilet. Dick wanted to leave his pants up, but Greg convinced him that that wouldn't be realistic. The audience wouldn't see "anything," it would be a quick scene, but he had to be naked, with his pants around his ankles. Shot from the hall, with the bathroom door slightly open, Greg's character bounds in, holding a toothbrush, only to find the bathroom occupied. Mr. Burns glares at him and Greg's character sheepishly apologizes before slinking off.

The first time, there was a focus problem. Greg carefully broke the news to Dick that the shot would need to be done again, and while obviously displeased, Dick agreed, relieved when it was done, and everyone seemed to think it looked funny. Then Bradley the camera-man called Greg over and suggested that it might be better if the dad said something in protest when Greg opened the door. Greg couldn't deny the humor that would create, he just wasn't sure how to cajole Dick into doing the scene just one more time. A good sport, Dick did so but used his real frustration on the next take when he said, "Hey!" which resulted in a huge laugh when audiences saw the scene.

The bathroom was used for another, more unsettling scene when they filmed the scene where the character of Greg overflowed the toilet. To get the right effect, yellow food coloring and some candy bars were added to the toilet water which, while it looked grosser than it sounds, was quite authentic for the purpose. The small bathroom meant Bradley had to stand in the tub to get the shot, but it turned out fine. The following scene, filmed right after, shows the family gathering outside the bathroom door, plunger in hand, much to Greg's embarrassment.

The next scene filmed using the bathroom concerned the family gathering outside the door worried about Fay who has locked herself in the bathroom after the character of Greg made the mistake of telling her she might benefit from taking a few more voice lessons. Irv is just about to break down the door when Fay emerges, mascara dripping down her face, and tells everyone how Greg went into her room the previous night and they had sex. Greg explains that he went in there by mistake, and nothing happened, but of course, they all believe Fay. Dick turns to Greg, saying, "You're a real prince, aren't you?" before stalking off. When everyone has left, Fay abruptly stops her crying, then gives Greg a conniving look that screams, "Ha ha!"

"I took that from my childhood," Greg said. "My younger sister, when we were kids, was crying to my dad that I pushed her off her bike. He yelled at me and walked away, then she stopped her tears and gave me the same look as Fay. Writers use everything!"

Upstairs in the Palatine house was also where they filmed the scene involving Greg knocking over Grandma's ashes. A scene right out of Greg's short "The Vase." In *Meet the Parents* the picture of Irv's late mother, Penny, is a photo of Greg's Aunt Pat taken specifically for this film. Aunt Pat played along wonderfully, slicking back her hair and painting her brows into a unibrow that highlighted the stern features she had for the photo. When it came time to break the urn, they put in it ashes transported last minute from Greg's sister's fireplace. The ashes, however, were still hot, the urn retaining the heat. They found this out on the drive back to the location and the container fell over, burning the crew members in the back seat.

One of the scenes on the schedule for the upstairs Palatine location occurs when Carol trips over Greg's bag and falls down the stairs. The end of that scene had already been filmed previously at the Wijas home so essentially, Mrs. Burns tripped in Palatine and ended up face down, at the foot of the stairs, in Park Ridge.

For scenes in Fay's bedroom, Mary Ruth channeled her inner Fay and decorated the room to look like a room she imagined the character, a show business hopeful, would have. There were pictures of Barbara Streisand and Judy Garland all over as well as cardboard stars, covered with tin foil on the walls. For the scene in which Greg tries to sneak into Pam's room but mistakenly goes into Fay's, he was supposed to hide under the bed, but the bed was too low, so Greg's closeup under the bed was done without a bed over him.

By interesting coincidence, the family who lived in the Palatine location house had a daughter who liked to sing so they asked if the crew would like to use the microphone and amplifier she had for Fay's song "When Phillip's There." That was a big yes. The original plan was to have her sing it with just the accompaniment on tape, but having the amp with the feedback, and Mary Ruth holding a microphone made it even more real. The problem with the scene was the production was on its last role of film and Brad estimated there was about seven- or eight-minutes left. Luckily, Greg's side of the scene had already been filmed, but Fay's whole song and the scene where she coaxes a criticism out of Greg and then flips out might just run that long. Greg pulled Mary Ruth aside and explained the situation, telling her to imagine that she was live on stage and if she made a mistake, she should keep going. As a theater actress, this would not be a problem for her, and she performed the entire scene, song, dialogue, and flip out in the time allotted.

With that, filming for *Meet the Parents* was at last complete.

This is the One!

Greg was happy for the quick shoot since the longer a low-budget shoot goes on, the more things tend to fall apart. But now it was time to see exactly what they had. They wouldn't be sure until after the film was cut together, but he'd been happy with the performances. Emo Philips was also interested in seeing just what he'd invested in. Greg picked the long take of Mary Ruth singing "When Phillip's There" since it could be appreciated without editing. Also, Emo had never heard the song even though he knew about it, and suggested it be placed in a section where there are a lot of words performed quickly. Much to Greg's relief, when the scene started, Emo was in hysterics. He was the first person outside the cast and crew to see anything that was shot and judging by his reaction, it was a success.

The plan was to shoot on film, then transfer the film to video to edit, which Greg had done with most of his shorts. This was back in 1990 when video was still markedly inferior visually to film. Ultimately, they would have a final cut on ¾ inch videotape. Len Austrevich had a VHS editing deck that Greg rented from him, so all the rushes, once they were synced to sound, were transferred onto VHS tape. All the technical work, the developing, and sound syncing was done at a place called Swell Pictures.

Installing video equipment in his apartment, Greg was ready to start editing, finding it all fairly rudimentary. With only two tracks for sound, the problem would occur if he wanted a scene to have dialogue, music, and a sound effect. Once he mastered the art of editing on VHS, he edited it quickly, cutting five or six minutes together, then recutting after Jim saw it and gave him his notes. The need to do scenes in one take turned out to Greg's benefit since it made the editing simple, like putting a puzzle together. If a challenge arose, for example, if scenes didn't match, then Greg would need to get creative. When a reaction shot was needed for the father regarding something dumb the character of Greg has said, Greg, the filmmaker found a bit of film that was a closeup of Dick waiting on Greg the director to say "action." He cut in the deadpan reaction to Greg the character's dumb comment and it always got a big laugh when the film was screened.

Greg found that certain bits of music worked with the humor. For the gas station scenes where Jim is relating the story of Pam and Greg, Greg added ominous, horror movie music. That made a relatively normal scene funny. As a fan of sad, classical music, Greg realized how valuable it was, when played over comedy, to bring out the sense of mock tragedy. When the father asked if Greg broke his victrola, Chopin's sad piano "Prelude in E Minor Opus 28, No. 4" plays over the scene making it that much funnier.

As much as his creative juices were still flowing, the long hours of editing were burning him out. The first people to see a part of the film were friends from high school, Steve and Mary Jo Cubberly. Jim took over the first 30 minutes of the film for them to watch and reported back that they thought it was very funny. This made Greg even more determined to finish the edit. With no comedy shows booked that week, he edited for over 12 hours a day until within a week he, at last, had a rough cut that Jim signed off on. Despite the tape having a time code on the bottom of the screen, they decided to have a screening. Films are often screened for small sections of the public before the official release to gauge how they will play with an audience. That way anything that may need tweaking before the general release can be done. Greg's days in standup taught him how valuable listening to the audience was when honing comedy.

A screening was arranged at a place called The Roxy, on Fullerton Avenue, in Chicago. It had a bar and a small stage area that seated around 50 people, but the club also had a screen where Greg and Jim could project the VHS tape. Cast and crew members were asked to invite people and by Oct. 16, they had a decent-sized audience to screen the film. Despite having the timecode on the bottom, none of the colors adjusted, and poor, two-track sound, the film played great with nice laughs throughout. "I remember my brother-in-law Tim came with my sister Vickie," Greg stated. "I respected their opinion, and they sincerely seemed to like it. I remember Tim, who was a very funny guy, saying to me with a serious expression, 'This is the one!'"

The screening proved to be valuable. According to Greg, "I had not, until that night, realized how ahead of us the audience was. Once they figured out the 'game' (Greg inadvertently does innocent things and fate conspires to turn them into disasters) they were second guessing everything."

The trick was to have them not see the gag coming. In the first draft, the second the character of Greg threw the stick into the water for the dog to fetch, the audience groaned realizing the dog wasn't long for this world. When he goes into the room with the grandmother's urn and begins waving his arms, the audience knew what was coming next. The screening also illustrated that some exterior shots were missing. And some little bits were needed to help the narrative progress. They hadn't made it clear, for example, that Fay had sabotaged Greg's car to keep him from leaving before she could sing to him, so a shot was needed to show her tampering with it. A close-up of Fay's deranged look when Greg first offered a critique of her singing was needed. The scene where Pam and Greg rise from the sofa in shock was not big enough, after hearing how big a scream it got when Mom walks onscreen with her eye and half her face covered in tape. They needed to redo that.

The bottom line was that additional filming was needed and that meant going back to Emo for more money. They figured that another $10,000 was needed for reshoots and to put together a finished tape. After hearing how well the screening went despite these issues, Emo readily agreed to give them the extra money.

But reshoots were not going to be easy. Reshooting Pam and Greg's reactions to Mrs. Burns' eyepatch meant going back to the Wijas house to shoot in her living room. Sybil, however, had just repainted that room and now it was a different color (though whether she did it to keep the crew from coming back is a matter for debate). She did allow them to film the exterior of her house, but a month had passed, and shooting on Nov. 26 turned out to be a cold experience. Luckily, Steve and Mary Jo Cubberly had a wall in their house that matched the original house perfectly. So, Sybil let the production borrow the painting that was behind the characters originally when the scene was filmed in her house to hang in the Cubberly house. The Cubberly couch, however, was not the right-sized couch, so Jacqueline Cahill and Greg ended up sitting on boxes, then rising to their feet to react to the eye injury.

Since the scene where Greg broke the urn was going to be redone, Greg the filmmaker decided to go for a creepier, darker look than the original room possessed with its white walls. Jim suggested finding a funeral home and the owners of Symonds Funeral Home in Chicago were game to let them film. It had a small room that was perfect, full of dark brown wood with reverential lighting that fit the father's obsessive admiration for his late mom. The next trick was to figure out how Greg breaks the urn without the gag being telegraphed to the audience beforehand in the movie. He decided that he would enter the room to talk to Pam, waving his arms around excitedly, nearly missing knocking over the urn. Then, just when the audience decided he wasn't going to knock it over, he would leave the room and close the door hard, causing the picture of Grandma to fall off the wall, knocking over the urn and sending ash into the air.

That was a complicated shot to get. "Someone held the picture on the wall, crouched low so we never saw them in the shot," Greg explained. "And someone operating a small fan, who was also on the floor off-camera. When I shut the door, the stagehand caused the picture to fall forward and the fan was turned on, shooting ash upward." The funeral home got involved when, curiously, they allowed the production to use someone's unclaimed ashes. "Every funeral home has ashes that no one picked up stored in cardboard boxes. I wondered whose ashes we were putting on screen, but whoever they were, we didn't get a release from them. I like to think they were someone who had always dreamed of being in the movies."

After concluding at the funeral home, more shots were needed of Mary Ruth. Greg had decided they were missing a close-up of her in full crazy mode. All they had were the bravura long take and the medium shot. Luckily, since it was a close-up, they wouldn't need to go back to the second-floor location, so they did it at Mary Ruth's apartment. They also got a shot of her putting something obviously from a car's engine into a drawer, which would set up the fact that she had toyed with Greg's car to keep him from leaving. This addressed the issue of people asking at the screening, "Why didn't the car start?"

Once the new shots were developed and put on video, the new scenes were cut into the film. Greg was scheduled to open for Emo at the West Palm Beach Comedy Center in a few weeks, and there was an adjoining theater, so Emo arranged to have a screening of the film there, after the show.

The week before Christmas, 1990, music was recorded for the film. They liked the idea of Fay singing "When Phillip's There" with an orchestra and wild applause over the closing credits so that was recorded. Scott May, a house musician for The Funny Firm who'd also played with the Chicago band, The Ides of March, and had done music for *They Came from Next Door* did the honors. Also recorded was a track of Greg's song "Keep Smiling," sung by Greg's friend Walter Tabayoyong which is heard when he's driving the dad's car. The final song recorded was the title song "Meet the Parents." The song is sung by Mary Louise Herrold, and for that one, they chose an arrangement similar to an old Doris Day song called "Everybody Loves a Lover."

That New Year's Eve, Greg found himself driving up to a comedy gig in Libertyville, Illinois, accompanied on the trip by thoughts of his latest film project; one so much more elaborate than the shorts he'd made or even his first feature, *They Came from Next Door*. It had indeed been two weeks of hell, but it had also been exhilarating and creatively satisfying in a way that his stand-up act no longer was. And unlike the comedic monologues he'd performed for audiences over the years, *Meet the Parents* was a tangible thing. Something he could refer back to.

The test screening indicated how successful it could be. Now that it was newly edited, how much more favorable might the reception be? His past film work had led to it. Would *Meet the Parents* also lead to future film work for him? While comedy had been fun in the beginning, Greg had been questioning his choice of profession for some time by that point. "I was getting tired of spending New Year's Days driving home from some gig. I was hoping this film would rescue me from the life of a standup comic."

On Jan. 15, 1991, after Greg and Emo finished their sets at a comedy club up north, Emo invited anyone interested to go next door to watch the premiere of a new comedy film. Admission was free. About 50 people turned up to watch the film with the new footage. None of the sound or picture had been corrected and the print still had the time code at the bottom which they asked the audience to ignore. But they didn't elaborate on those issues either. Emo once told Greg, "You could show a perfect film to an audience save for one frame that had a dinosaur in it. You could ask people to ignore the dinosaur and they would agree. Then afterward, when asked how they liked the film, they'd answer, 'Well, there was this dinosaur…'"

Despite those issues, the film went over like gangbusters, the new scenes helping dramatically, and Emo and Greg were both thrilled with the response.

While the audience was incredibly receptive to the print they saw, the film still needed to be finalized. The production team made a deal with a company owned by Jack Liga called VPA Teleproductions, located in Des Plaines. They liked the film and offered a good deal, which kept to the new budget of $40,000. The idea was to use the timecode numbers to cut the tale onto a one-inch master. That's when it was decided to use actual photos of people's parents for the opening credits and everyone involved was asked to bring pictures of their families, allowing the producers to choose the ones they wanted to use. Then it came time to adjust the picture qualities, looking at each shot to adjust the colors and brightness to fit the tone of the film. Since Greg's main idea about it was that it was a horror film, he didn't want it to look too cheerful and bright. There needed to be a sense of doom. They took care of that at Allied Film and Video in Chicago and did sound editing at Zenith/DB studios in Chicago.

By Feb. 26, 1991, they had a finished print for another showing at The Roxy. "I don't want to brag," Greg remembered, "but it went over like we had come to expect. It was not a perfect, classic comedy, but if you showed it to an audience, you heard giant laughs."

The question was what to do now? The logical thing would be to get a distributor, so Greg and Jim decided to have a press screening to see what critics thought of it and to hopefully get a few quotes to use for promotional packets. A small screening room was booked at what at the time was Oprah Winfrey's Harpo Studios on Washington Boulevard in Chicago. To their dismay, only one of the critics they invited, Dave Kehr of the Chicago Tribune, showed up. Greg often found himself agreeing with his reviews, but he knew that seeing a movie alone in an otherwise empty theater was not the best way to see a comedy. Too nervous to watch it with him, Greg waited outside, sneaking in only once to note his reactions. "He would occasionally write something down in a notepad and once I saw him chuckling to himself, which I was very happy to see."

Playing it cool, Greg and Jim thanked him for coming and he left without giving them a quote or any indication of whether he liked it. Then they went out for coffee and discussed their options which unfortunately were limited. Back in '91, there wasn't a plethora of film festivals the way there is now, and the independent scene was not nearly as vibrant as it would be in a few years with the rise of film makers like Kevin Smith and Quentin Tarantino. A direct-to-video possibility might be just the thing, but where to start?

What they didn't know was that Emo had taken a step on his own.

Enter Lampoon

National Lampoon had its humble beginnings in the *Harvard Lampoon*, which began in 1876 as a campus humor magazine inspired by the British magazine *Punch*. As the decades wore on, it became notable for its parodies of popular periodicals such as *Esquire. Mademoiselle, Playboy, Time,* and *Life*. A 70-page parody of a James Bond novel titled *Alligator* would lead to future novel parodies including *Bored of the Rings*, a spoof of Tolkein's *Lord of the Rings* published in 1969. Written by Douglas Kenny and Henry Beard, editors of the Harvard Lampoon, the massive success of *Bored of the Rings* inspired Kenny and Beard, along with Robert Hoffman to start *National Lampoon Magazine*, sort of an off shoot of the *Harvard Lampoon* from which they licensed the name in 1969.

Where the *Harvard Lampoon* remained a college magazine, *National Lampoon* purposely reached beyond college to much broader social issues of the day often addressing them with risqué humor that pushed the envelope. It also had writing and artwork from some of the premiere humorists of the time including Michael O'Donoghue, Anne Beatts, and John Hughes.

The success of the magazine brought about for the Lampoon brand forays into other media including the stage show *National Lampoon's Lemmings* and the *National Lampoon Radio Show*, both featuring up-and-coming names in comedy like John Belushi, Gilda Radner, Dan Akroyd, and Bill Murray.

It is perhaps the success of their movies that has left the most lasting impression on the public. The first feature film produced under the brand was *National Lampoon's Animal House* in 1978. Written, directed, and performed by many people long associated with Lampoon's other projects, *Animal House* became a hit that helped broaden National Lampoon's appeal and spawned a whole new genre of similar movies.

Other movies with the National Lampoon label would follow, most notably *National Lampoon's Vacation* (1983) and *Christmas Vacation* (1989), and it seemed that the popularity of the movies might take over for the magazine, which at that point had begun to flounder.

Unfortunately, National Lampoon's movie division was showing signs of drying up both creatively and success-wise. The pool of comedic talent that had made its many creative endeavors so successful had gone on to other opportunities. It was long felt among the staff of Lampoon that National Lampoon helped make *Saturday Night Live* since so many of the Not Ready for Prime Time Players, and the writers that wrote for them got their start with either the Lampoon magazine, stage production, or radio show.

A name that at one time had been associated with relevant, edgy humor was now thought of as a purveyor of low-brow, gross-out humor and internal struggles at the magazine were tarnishing the brand. James P. Jimirro, CEO of J2 Communications hoped to change that. J2 had purchased National Lampoon in 1991 from partners Daniel Grodnik and Tim Matheson (one of the stars of *Animal House*) who themselves had grabbed the reins after a hostile takeover of the magazine in 1989. That purchase gained both the magazine and the rights to the name, which Jimirro planned to license out to a variety of entertainment projects including cruises, and even a themed restaurant. His big interest seemed to be getting the movie division back on track.

Jimirro, the creator of the Disney Channel and a one-time CBS executive, founded J2 Communications in 1986. The company had a great deal of success in the burgeoning direct-to-video market, its most notable product at the time being the Tim Conway *Dorf* videos. While success for National Lampoon's theatrically released movies was waning, Jimirro was certain that the legendary comedy brand could regain its past glory with direct-to-video movies.

J2 started out of the gate strong with the release of *National Lampoon's Loaded Weapon*, a parody of the *Lethal Weapon* films, starring Emilio Estevez and Samuel L. Jackson. The movie was a success at the box office, but subsequent films did not fare as well, and, when he took over, Jimirro was wondering if perhaps it was time to take a different tack with the Lampoon films. Starting by opening them up to a more diverse audience than college frat boys. A low-budget indie film had landed on his desk one day after Brenton Levy, then a lawyer for Emo Philips sent out copies of *Meet the Parents* to various companies in the hopes of finding a distributor for the film. According to what Jimirro later told Greg, when he brought the film home to watch with his wife, he looked across at her and saw her doubled over with laughter. He had a feeling that this little film might be exactly what he needed to retain the comedic edge yet bring a little sophistication to the brand. So, he made the team an offer.

Of course, Greg, Jim, and Emo couldn't believe their luck. Right out of the starting gate this movie was going to be associated with one of the legendary names of comedy. The film's new title would be *National Lampoon's Meet the Parents*, bringing with it all the cache of the brand.

"It seemed almost too good to be true," Greg remembered. "Jim and I didn't celebrate until a contract was signed by all parties. When that happened, we went out to dinner and toasted our good fortune."

Greg was also thrilled with the possibility that this might open doors for more movies to be filmed in Chicago. Setting up CEM Productions, he began to envisage the possibilities of future projects produced by his production company. He was just finishing up a script that involved the loss of a winning lottery ticket and the covering up of an affair. Perhaps that movie could be another offering in The National Lampoon line of video movie releases. (Later, Greg would cut the concept for that movie into two scripts: The lottery ticket idea which had never sold, and the infidelity story which would become *A Guy Thing* starring Jason Lee and Julia Styles).

To make the news even sweeter, Dave Kehr, the lone critic who attended the screening at the Roxy, told a contact at the Art Institute of Chicago about the film and the Film Center of the prestigious institution reached out to arrange a screening. Though the movie was due to be released on video that fall, how could they pass up a screening at the Art Institute of Chicago? They booked it for July 19, 1991.

Lampoon gave Greg and Jim $5,000 as an advance for the project. Greg intended to honor his deal with Emo so that the comic would receive back his initial investment from any profits of the film, then future profits could be split. But Emo allowed Greg to keep his advance for which Greg, who, financially, was living week to week, was grateful.

In the meantime, they prepared for the July 19 showing of *Meet the Parents* at the Film Center. Dave Kehr continued his support for the film by writing a nice little blurb about it that appeared in the Chicago Tribune. It was their first review:

"Local comedy of a very different kind is on display in 'Meet the Parents', a 78-minute video feature receiving its premiers at 6 and 8:30 p.m. Friday at the Film Center of the School of the Art Institute. Directed by Greg Glienna, the film might be described as cornfield Kafka—a sunny Midwestern black comedy in which the setting is an idyllic small town, the characters are kind and well-meaning, and the sense of entrapment and helplessness is overwhelming. Glienna, with the deadest of deadpans, plays the protagonist, a young Chicagoan who drives to Indiana with his fiancé (Jackie Cahill) for his all-important first meeting with his future in-laws. Before the weekend is over, he has drowned the family dog, put out his mother-in-law's eye with a fishing rod, and been serenaded by his fiancée's sister, an amateur singer who will stop at nothing to get on 'Star Search.' Shooting in a slow, patient, painfully naturalistic style, Glienna creates his humor by capping disaster with disaster, coming up with ever more perverse and imaginative ways to torture and humiliate his silently suffering hero. Emo Phillips, who served as the film's executive producer, appears in a short, funny bit as an eccentric video-store clerk, but the sensibility of the film is Glienna's own. It's a very funny, original piece of work."

The theater was packed for both shows and Jim, Emo, and Greg went out afterward to answer questions, including the one that would soon be a staple of every future screening, "How did you get the dog to sniff your crotch?" After the questions, they were approached by Sandy Chaney, manager of the Music Box Theatre, one of the most successful and esteemed art houses in Chicago. Expressing his love for the film, Chaney told the crew that he'd be happy to arrange a showing at the Music Box. While the team was honored by the offer, they declined, concerned that a showing might cause a conflict with the fall release of the film on video only months away. Nevertheless, it was an exciting offer and made them realize how much potential the film carried.

This did cause Greg a slight pang of regret. As happy as he was with the Lampoon deal, seeing the film with an audience at the Film Center made him wonder if the movie could have a theatrical release instead of premiering on video. Comedies were so much stronger when seen with an audience.

Still, the Lampoon deal was a good opportunity, and he couldn't help but be excited when a full-page ad for the movie ran in the current issue of National Lampoon Magazine. The film's budget had not allowed for an on-set photographer (a problem easily solved today by smart phones), so the stills from the movie used in the ad were made from the master tape. While the shots were grainy, they still did the trick. At the bottom of the ad, it stated, "Greg's about to become an in-law" with the word "in" crossed out and the word "out" scribbled in its place. Below that, it proclaimed, "Coming to home video this Fall."

A page-and-a-half press release from Lampoon even had a pre-book date of Sept. 18, 1991, a release date of Oct. 9, 1991, and a suggested retail price of $19.95.

Adding to the excitement of the time, the team encountered the Holy Grail of the independent film world: An investor! Neither Jim nor Greg can remember how they met this man, nor, for that matter, can they remember his first name. Greg refers to him simply as The Investor. He was a successful businessman heading up a consortium of successful businessmen looking to get into the film racket.

While The Investor wasn't certain about the dependability of investing in this movie, he was a fan of the film and was very impressed that National Lampoon was releasing it. Over the course of several dinners, Jim and Greg discussed *Meet the Parents* as well as the new script which Greg was calling *The Big Prize*. The Investor looked over the Lampoon contract, calculating how much would be made if the film was a reasonable hit, and Greg explained that it was just the beginning. Future films didn't have to be limited to home video release. Money could be made from both a theatrical release and a home video release. A young film maker with plenty of ideas, Greg revealed his dream of starting a film company in Chicago and releasing a film per year.

"It looked like the beginning of a beautiful friendship," Greg said. "I was walking on air at this time. I played a comedy club out of state and there was a walk where comedians signed their names. I remember writing my name and adding, 'Before *Meet the Parents* came out.' Of course, in life, the wise man starts to worry, not when everything's bad but when everything is going well."

Exit Lampoon

There's a particular heartbreak to seeing your dreams crash and burn especially when it's through no fault of your own. Before the rise of digital convenience, to get their work out to the public, a creator had to rely on the help of others, backers, investors, and mentors, which meant they had to rely on the honesty and willingness of those people to see the project through. In business, a person's word is only as strong as their commitment to the project, and sometimes that commitment can burn away fast.

As August rolled around, Greg, Jim, and Emo were beginning to get nervous. The release of the video was supposedly weeks away, but communications from Jimirro and Lampoon had grown sporadic at best. They noticed also that Lampoon hadn't put ads for the film in the latest issue of the magazine. When Greg called Lampoon, he was reassured that everything was on track, but when fall came, the movie still hadn't been released. Eventually, Lampoon informed them that they had given the video cassette of *Meet the Parents* to some college kids, presumably to watch in their dorms, and the results were not what they were hoping for. "The kids said that the film wasn't what they expected from the National Lampoon brand," said Greg. "I guess Jim Jimirro had forgotten his initial desire to expand the brand from gross-out, slapstick comedy to more mainstream. In the meantime, our investor called to ask why the film had not been released and was told it was delayed, but to the best of our knowledge it was going to happen."

Lampoon finally called with a possible solution: What if Emo recorded an introduction to the film, where he explained how this was going to be a different comedy film than they might be expecting? Of course, the funnier the better. As a marketing tool, it came off as a bit desperate. Still, the team came up with an idea in which

Emo could begin the piece by giving a serious talk about what the film didn't include, like pies in the face and people getting hit in the head with boards all the while performing these very gags. ("The secret," he informed the audiences in solemn tones, "is to put your hand up to your forehead to block the blow"). The video was completed, ending with Emo getting a pie in the face, but the team wasn't completely happy with the result. Plus, such a broad introduction to a movie with such subtle comedy seemed too extreme a dichotomy.

They sent it to Lampoon anyway but didn't get a response to it. Eventually, the company let them know that Lampoon wouldn't be releasing the film. "The story we were told," Greg said, "was that they had signed a deal with New Line Pictures to release some low-budget movies, but not as low as our budget, that's for sure, and New Line wasn't happy about our little micro-budget film being on the shelves next to their more expensive, studio films. Films like *National Lampoon's Loaded Weapon 1*, which has a rating of 18% on Rotten Tomatoes, and *National Lampoon's Senior Trip*, which wasn't even reviewed enough to get a rating."

According to Emo, it was like J2 Communications, who had acquired the Lampoon brand, "...had bought a classic Rolls Royce automobile and then ran it into a brick wall destroying it."

"They gave us the use of the artwork they had commissioned," Greg said, "which we used for our official poster, in exchange, I guess, for us not suing them."

It was a bold idea on the part of Jim Jimirro to try to open up a brand that had long been become associated with college humor of the base kind to a larger audience. Perhaps, considering how J2 Communications had just recently taken over the brand, it was too bold a move to attempt until things had settled down after the purchase. But attempt it they did, though unfortunately, the execution wasn't nearly as bold as the decision itself. To offer for review a movie that you hope is the seed that will help grow a wider audience only to representatives of the demographic from which you're trying to expand makes absolutely no sense. And it raises the question of how committed Jimirro and J2 were to the plan, to begin with.

Lampoon was out $5,000 and some artwork, while their prematurely aborted experiment with changing their image cost Greg and his friends the valuable time they could have spent looking for a distributor willing to honor a contract.

Lampoon pulling out of the deal also cost CEM Productions their investor who had been uncertain about the film business, to begin with.

"I'm not usually a person who enjoys looking back," Greg said, "but thinking about this time, I can easily remember how depressing this news was. For me, it's one of those 'What if?' moments that almost everyone experiences in their lifetimes. If Lampoon had released our film, I'm sure it would have done well. Maybe it would have caused some resentment from fans of the brand, but I do believe it would have reached the people who genuinely seemed to 'get' the film and been something of a cult film. We would have gone ahead, most likely with the next film from CEM Productions. It was a funny script. I may have also had a career as an actor, which I think I'm good at, though I've never had the desire to pursue the actor's life, with all that entails. What I could have had was a shot at making my own films in Chicago, which was a dream of mine. But as the saying goes, 'Man makes plans, God laughs.'"

With no other distributors expressing interest in releasing the movie, Emo, Jim and Greg considered their options. The screenings had shown that there was most definitely an audience for it. And they remembered the offer of Sandy Chaney, manager of the Music Box Theater, to show the film there. With the reputation of the Music Box in the arts community, if the film was a success, it might attract distributors. The only problem was that to show it there they'd need a film print. Everything had been transferred from 16 mm to video, then edited on video to make the final print. Which meant they'd essentially have to go back to the film stock and edit the film all over again. This would cause a budget that had already increased a few times to balloon even further. Emo, to the rescue again, was willing to put up the money, joking later that he put $35,000 of his savings into the film, and he tripled his investment...he later had to put another $70,000 into it!

A little money could be saved by using the existing soundtrack of the video, which had been mixed and balanced, with music and sound effects, cutting the film to match the sound. "This meant that we couldn't get back the footage that we had cut on the wishes of National Lampoon, which left us with a shorter-than-average running time. We decided we would show the short film I had directed for Emo, 'The Can Man,' as an added attraction."

In the meantime, Greg alternated stand-up comedy with gigs singing at piano bars after having gone with a friend to an open mic night at a piano bar on Halsted Street in Chicago called The Gentry. His mother had done some professional singing when she was young and even recorded a song titled "Getting a Man Takes a Plan" in the '60s and that talent rubbed off on her son. At The Gentry, he sang and played and went over very well, which encouraged him to continue going every Sunday to the open mics hosted by a talented pianist and singer named Beckie Menzie. Eventually, the owner asked if he wanted to perform there regularly, and he continues to do so whenever he's in town.

The Music Box

Built in 1929, The Music Box Theater on North Southport Avenue seated 750 people making it a small theater at a time when movie palaces were being built to accommodate a couple of thousand. Unlike those palaces, built to present both movies and live shows, The Music Box was built purely for the love of film. Its size was part of its charm. The theater soldiered on through the decades when the advent of TV hit the movie business hard, but by the late 70s and early 80s, it was pretty much being used to show Spanish and Arabic language films and even the odd porno. In 1983, the Music Box Theatre Corporation formed by Chaney, Christopher Carlo, and Stan Hightower restored it and opened it up to double features, foreign films, cult films, and independent films in keeping with the vibrancy of Chicago's creative scene. In 1991, a smaller theater seating 100 was built in an empty storefront next to the lobby. That was the theater where *Meet the Parents* would open on April 3, 1992.

This offered plenty of time to edit the film as well as hire a publicist and make a poster. Using the Lampoon artwork, they had to do a bit of censoring since the Lampoon artwork had Mary Ruth's arms around Greg's right thigh and his pants unzipped (perhaps indicating what the Lampoon mindset on the movie had been all along). They decided to cover up the unzipped pants, so people didn't think it was...well a National Lampoon film. Advances in technology have made such design work easier, but at the time, it meant a trip to Kinko's Copies Center for an evening of physical cutting and pasting with scissors and glue. The woman they hired to do publicity was able to get a fair amount of press: Articles in local papers, gigs on the radio, and Jim and Greg did an early morning TV news show on a local channel.

The week of April 3rd rolled around, and reviews started to appear in the local press. Dave Kehr backed the film again calling it "hip comedy" and stating that "while the production values are fairly minimal, it does possess the tremendous asset of fresh, original comic sensibility."

So fond of the film was Kehr that, ten years later, at the opening of the Gene Siskel Film Theater in Chicago, some local movie reviewers were asked to choose their favorite movie filmed in Chicago for a screening and he chose *Meet the Parents*.

Dan Gire gave it three out of four stars in the *Daily Herald*, acknowledging the "suburbanized domestic horror tale" of the story and calling it a "marvelous example of deadpan, dead-on comic tone that allows the humor to seep out from the theater screen, instead of hitting us over the head in standard sit-com style."

Kevin Sweeney of the Lerner Newspapers gave the film three stars calling it a "highly original nightmare comedy of embarrassment as long as it focuses on Greg's unwilling dismantling of the parents' lives."

A particular favorite of Greg's, due to his affinity for Woody Allen, is a review by Peter Sobczynski in *Inferno Magazine* in which the reviewer alludes to both *Parents*, and Allen's then-recently released *Shadows and Fog*, proclaiming *Parents* to be the superior picture, stating that, "Watching these films back-to-back illustrates that having all the style in the world means nothing if one has nothing to say." He even compares it to Martin Scorsese's *After Hours*, "in that it's an extremely tense and strange comedy" and feels that Fay's musical number at the end "has shades of Lynch's *Eraserhead*."

Even *The Reader*, a weekly free newspaper with a reputation for being tough in reviews, especially for comedies, had critic Jonathan Rosenbaum naming it his Critic's Choice for the week, writing about the film's, "cascade of nightmares that may not always make you laugh but will impress you with the singularity of Glienna's dark approach...and the purity and relentlessness of this picture's vision."

Earnest Tucker of the *Chicago Sun-Times* also gave it three stars, calling it a "witty surprise, a locally produced, low-budget black comedy that makes the most of its small scale." While John Petrakis of *Newcity*, another weekly free newspaper praised the movie for playing the comedy straight which, "is what makes *Meet the Parents* funnier than it should be."

More exciting, a local television station's news team came to the theater to cover the opening night. The two shows on Friday and two on Saturday were sold out, bringing the opening weekend box office to $6,486. According to what Sandy Chaney had expressed, he was sure that "had the theater been big enough to accommodate the turn-away crowds," the movie might have taken in $7,500 easily. Opening week, with limited showings, the film made $10,268. Not bad for a small film that had been edited and reedited and kicking around for nearly two years.

Greg snuck into the theater to listen to the audience's reaction, thrilled by the response, and Emo even recorded a showing on cassette tape so they could study in detail where the laughs were. "One thing Emo couldn't understand," Greg stated, "was why the audience laughed when, after his character speaks to me, the camera cuts to my character just looking blankly at his character. I told him I think it's because I looked at him honestly, the way a real person would look at someone who talked in a sing-songy cadence the way he spoke when in character."

One of the ushers told Greg that he saw a lot of people coming back for a second or third viewing and once, while Greg was out in front taking photos of the marquis, he was excited to hear two girls stop in front of the poster, one telling the other, "I heard this was really funny." Word of mouth was spreading. He was even recognized at Kinko's while photo-copying material for the film. "Aren't you in that movie *Meet the Parents*?" someone asked. And this wasn't even in the same neighborhood as the Music Box.

Of course, these positive reviews buoyed Greg's spirits after the debacle with National Lampoon and strengthened his belief that the film had potential as a theatrical release. It was just a matter of finding a distributor who had faith in it as well.

Missionaries

Emo once made the comment that *Meet the Parents* seemed to attract "missionaries" who after viewing the film acquired a sincere belief in it and wanted to help Greg, Jim, and Emo make it a success. Sandy Chaney was one such person. Seeing the response to the Music Box screenings he used his connections to get the movie booked at a theater in Atlanta where it played for a week. During that time, Greg received a phone call from a woman who tracked him down to tell him how much she loved the film. She was trying to spread the news in Atlanta and offered to help in any way she could. "It caught me off guard, but it was nice to hear," Greg said.

The biggest problem when it came to distribution became clearer during this time. The film was too low budget to interest the bigger theaters, yet a tough sell in the arthouse market because it was a comedy. "Our patrons don't like comedies," theater owners would tell Sandy who would assure them that it wasn't a typical comedy and explain how well it did at the Music Box. Unfortunately, he didn't have much luck in changing their minds.

Perhaps one of the greatest "missionaries," if not for the result but for heart, was a man named Clay Heery, a friend of Emo from the comedy world.

Clay Heery was, by his own admission, a failed comic. "I started out as a very, very bad comic in Philadelphia." Bad comedian though he may be, he was nonetheless an earnest one and worked anywhere he could get on a stage be it bars, strip clubs, or gas stations. Sometimes he brought milk crates and a board and made his own stage depending on the venue. To be fair, at the time the Philadelphia area had no major comedy scene and it's difficult to hone one's craft when there's nowhere available to hone one's craft. Eventually, Clay decided to switch hats and leave the life of a comic for that of a comedy club owner. A career for which he seemed much better suited. Opening the Comedy Factory Outlet in downtown Philadelphia, he became known as a "comic's club owner." Having done his tour of duty in the stand-up world, he knew what the life of a comic could be like. And found himself an advocate for the comics who played his clubs.

"I was the guy who was always on the side of the comics," he explained. "A lot of club owners weren't. They liked to abuse the comics."

But because there was no real home-grown comedy scene in the area, Clay found himself frequently having to go outside of Philadelphia to get extra comics to perform at his clubs. That's how he met a young comic from Chicago named Emo Phillips. A lot of comics performing at clubs spent a good portion of time fixating on how many seats were filled since, at the time, they were often paid for a percentage of the cover charge total. Hoping to encourage the comics to concentrate more on their act and less on selling out, Clay came up with what he called the "Door Deal." Simply, he got the total of the bar, and the comics got the total of the door. If a comic could only convince 10 people to come out and see his act, it would still be a low take-home. But at least the comic didn't have to split that low figure with the house.

One night, Emo, who at this point in his career was quite a draw, had sold out the house so Clay was happy to present him with a fairly high take from the door. Until he discovered that members of his staff had miscounted, and they were eight seats short of selling out. Still, Clay felt obligated to let Emo keep the amount he'd been given (and as it turned out later, there had been some walk-ins so that made up the eight-seat difference). This cemented Clay's reputation as a respectable club owner in the eyes of Emo and the two became friends.

Eventually, Clay opened Comedy Factory Outlets in Baltimore and Washington D.C. and the clubs were very successful. Unfortunately, Clay's marriage wasn't. As part of the divorce settlement, he was forced to sell the clubs. Once that was done, he decided it was time to pursue yet another career path, so he moved out west, to Los Angeles because, as he put it, "That's where show business lives," and started putting deals together in Hollywood. In 1986, he had engineered a video concert deal with Andrew Dice Clay, a hot comic at the time, video-taped at the Comedy Factory Outlet. It was a deal that still offers him residuals to this day. So why not see if he could do with other deals what he did with Andrew Dice Clay?

Knowing how successful he had been making that deal, Emo approached him and told him a story about a movie he'd financed called *Meet the Parents*. This was not long after National Lampoon dropped *Meet the Parents* and the comic was still stinging from that. According to Clay, Emo told him, "Look, I got this movie here and I think I've been ripped off about it. And I think if it were remade with a bigger budget, it could go places. Have a look at it."

Intrigued, Clay took the cassette Emo offered and immediately fell in love with the film.

He grasped the universality of the plot and appreciated the slow build-up to the comedic disaster. "Everybody feels so uncomfortable when they're meeting the parents for the first time. And it was the tick-tock of that clock, as everything starts going wrong that got me. It got into my bones."

Clay Heery had indeed become a missionary for the movie and approached the task of marketing it with missionary zeal. What he had was a low-budget movie that had a low budget for marketing, but Clay tried his best to work with it. Before the days of email, one relied on telephone books and phone calls to get the word out about creative projects. Clay happened to have a directory of movie studios and the contact numbers for their representatives. He also just happened to have a fax machine, a piece of office equipment that just recently found popularity among general consumers. Both would aid him in his quest. Using some of the marketing material left over from the National Lampoon disappointment, he put together a press kit featuring a synopsis of the movie, reviews, and a cover sheet with the movie logo and his contact info.

From 11 p.m. (phone rates went down after 11 o'clock) till two or three in the morning, Clay faxed away. Then the next morning, he fielded calls from studio representatives interested in viewing the movie. He received a pretty good return on his time investment and began setting up times to bring the movie to the studios. "This was the time of *El Mariachi,* and everyone was looking for low-budget deals."

Around this time, filmmaker Robert Rodriguez had a surprise hit with his film *El Mariachi,* made on a $7,000 budget originally intended for the Mexican home video market. When it caught the attention of Columbia Pictures, the film studio was willing to take a chance and bought the American rights, spending a couple hundred thousand dollars on transferring the film from 16 mm to 35 mm and a further couple million on distribution. It was a wise investment. While Columbia broke even with what they spent to distribute the film, the ensuing sequels would bring up the total for what would become known as the *El Mariachi* franchise to almost $125,000,000 on a total production budget of $36,007,000. Not a bad return in the long run.

This likely inspired other studios to sniff around for those low-budget gems in the burgeoning independent feature market that could either be remade into huge box-office hits or spawn sequels that could be.

Paramount Pictures was the first studio with which Clay arranged a screening. It may have been easier simply to drop off a cassette of the film, but according to Clay, "The director insisted that screenings had to be off the print because people don't appreciate comedy on cassette. They pause and look at it. It has to be shown in a theater where people laugh."

The director he referred to, of course, is Greg who doesn't recall making such a stipulation. It would be believable if he had though. Greg understood that comedy has a rhythm that can be thrown off by people pausing the video to go get another drink or to have a conversation. Theater goers are more likely to engage in the shared experience of laughter more than those watching at home with all its distractions. Watching a movie in a darkened theater allows for more focus and more emersion into the experience. Especially a film like *Meet the Parents* with a pace that incorporated a slow buildup of tension.

Whether he was told to or not, Clay took the canister of film and a bunch of press kits lovingly crafted at Kinko's and drove over to his appointment at Paramount Pictures.

Paramount Pictures was originally a film distribution company started by W.W. Hodkinson in 1914. It distributed films made by Adolph Zukor's Famous Players Film Company founded in 1912 and Jesse Lasky Feature Plays founded in 1911. After Zukor began buying up stock in Paramount Pictures, eventually Famous Players merged with Jesse Lasky to form Famous Players-Lasky. The two bought (or pushed) Hodkinson out of Paramount and the three companies became one. Years later, The Paramount Famous Lasky Corporation would become simply Paramount Pictures, one of the most iconic film studios in the U.S.

Paramount had a small screening room that fit about 12 seats where no doubt the dailies of countless Hollywood blockbusters had been screened for executives checking on their progress. Each seat had its own phone. Scott Rudin had been the studio representative that arranged the screening, but when it was time to show the film, it was his assistant who sat in a seat in the screening room and prepared to view the picture. Up in the projectionist's booth, as the film began to roll, Clay looked down upon the young woman to gauge her reaction. He was dismayed to see that she spent most of the time talking on the phone.

"I'm thinking, 'What a bitch!' I almost stopped the screening." Clay admitted. "She's going to be on the phone the entire time and she's not paying any attention."

To Clay's surprise and relief, after the screening, he discovered that her phone conversation had not prevented the assistant from taking excellent notes. He felt confident she would represent the film well.

Sadly, despite the assistant's excellent notes, Paramount passed on the project.

Clay's next meeting was with Universal. As storied as Paramount, Universal Studios was founded in 1912 by Carl Laemmle, Mark Dintenfass, Charles O. Baumann, Adam Kessel, Pat Powers, William Swanson, David Horsley, Robert H. Cochrane, and Jules Brulatour, though for all intents and purposes the heart of the studio was Carl Laemmle (and later, Carl Laemmle Jr.). It was home to some of the most iconic monster movies ever created including the holy trinity of horror, *Dracula, Frankenstein,* and *The Wolfman.* The popularity of horror classics helped the studio survive the Great Depression during the 1930s. Universal didn't just produce horror movies, but when it did, it sure knew how to pick them.

With its fair share of comedy movies also under its belt, it wasn't a surprise that someone from Universal would contact Clay about *Meet the Parents.* Universal Studios was approximately 26 miles from his apartment in Marina De Rey. Driving all that way, dropping the movie off, driving back home, then driving back to pick up the movie would be a haul. So, after he dropped the movie off at the studio, Clay decided to slip into the Universal Theme Park right next door to occupy some time while the execs watched the film.

A few park rides and some concessions later, Clay decided to head back to the studio. The problem was that, while he could slip into the park from the studio, he couldn't slip back into the studio from the park. Instead, he had to walk about two miles back around to the entrance of the studio where a bemused guard listened to his story about needing to pick up a film and get back to his car parked on the studio lot. Having no doubt heard stranger stories, the guard allowed him entrance, and an exhausted and no doubt sunbaked Heery picked up the film and drove back to Marina del Rey.

Friends to whom he told the story questioned the wisdom of bothering with Universal at all considering the monster hit the studio just had with *Jurassic Park*. They probably wouldn't be interested in a small comedy.

Still, it seemed it had all been worth the slight inconvenience when, the next day, Universal called raving about the film. "Sure, comedies don't typically do well around the world," the rep told him enthusiastically, "but meeting the parents was something that could be understood around the globe. Despite the country or culture, your little film could have universal appeal."

Speaking of global appeal, Universal had indeed had a massive hit on its hands with *Jurassic Park*. At a budget of $63 million, the dinosaur movie based on Michael Crichton's novel of the same name grossed over $400 million in North America and over a billion worldwide. A triumph of visual effects combined with Steven Spielberg's masterful storytelling, the film would influence the industry and spawn two sequels and a reboot: *Jurassic World* which would spawn sequels of its own.

Dinosaurs had been very, very good to Universal and it's not unusual for a major movie studio to want to stick to a popular genre in the hopes that the money keeps rolling in. So perhaps it wasn't completely surprising when during their conversation, the rep for Universal made a very creative suggestion to Clay about *Meet the Parents*. "What if," Clay remembered him saying, "when Greg goes to meet the parents, he opens the door...and they're dinosaurs?"

It was not and would not be the first time a dinosaur comedy would come into play. Just a few years before, the sitcom *Dinosaurs*, featuring a family of dinosaurs set in a time when dinosaurs ruled the Earth (only this time they had mortgages and jobs), premiered and ran for four seasons on the ABC television network. And was pretty well received. Not so lucky was the film *Theodore Rex,* a buddy cop film starring Whoopi Goldberg and George Newbern as her partner Theodore Rex who also happens to be a Tyrannosaur (though not the 40-foot kind). Critics were not kind to this direct-to-video release.

Dinosaurs were in, but it's safe to say that in his hunt for a studio, knowing that a studio might want to make changes to the film, Clay never expected the sort of retconning idea that the Universal rep suggested. Though future dinosaur in-laws could indeed bring a whole new spin to meeting the parents.

Once Clay had picked his jaw off the floor, he told the rep that he would run the idea past Greg and Emo and see if they could imagine the possibilities. Neither of whom could, of course. And whether it was the kibosh being put on the dinosaur-in-laws or for some other reason, Universal ultimately passed on the film.

In the meantime, Clay was unsuccessfully working his way through contacts for Warner Brothers when New Line Cinema, a lower-budget division of Warner's showed some interest. There is some irony in this. New Line Productions, Inc. doing business as New Line Cinema began as a film distribution company in 1967. They mainly supplied foreign and art films to colleges. The company re-released the notorious and unintentionally hilarious 1936 anti-pot propaganda *Reefer Madness,* a favorite of college students everywhere. Many John Waters films were released by the studio, including his movie *Polyester,* as well as the horror film *Texas Chain Saw Massacre* which was re-released in 1983 by New Line after the original distributor, Bryanston Distributing Company lost the rights.

As time went on, New Line became more mainstream in its movies, producing films such as the *Nightmare on Elm Street movies, The Mask, Dumb and Dumber,* and *Rush Hour.* Later, the company would release mega-hits such as the *Austin Powers* movies, *The Lord of the Rings* series, and *The Conjuring*.

Being a low-budget division of studio giant Warner Brothers, the offices of New Line Cinema lacked the old Hollywood charm of the other movie studios Clay had been to. They didn't even have a screening room and told Clay that he would have to bring both a projector and a screen. Renting the equipment from a place in Venice, Clay drove the hour and some change for his 6 p.m. meeting with the reps at New Line. "Not a single one of them helped me," Clay remembered. "I'm carting this stuff, reels, projector, screen, and press kits, lugging it up in the elevator to the conference room, and not one of them lent a hand. They didn't even offer me water." It turned out that the conference room wasn't large enough for the screen to be set up, but the walls were white, so they were able to project the movie onto one of the walls.

The screening went well, and the execs expressed great enthusiasm for the film peppering Clay with questions. Unfortunately, by this time, tired, hungry, and knowing he still had to pack everything up before he could make the drive home, Clay's enthusiasm had waned. When asked what his vision was for the movie, Clay's patience snapped. "I don't have a fucking vision. Make the movie! It's a movie. You get it? He goes there, people die, this is the movie. Put it on screen, people pay money for it. This is what happens," is what he wanted to reply.

What he replied was a simple, "Look, it's 11 o'clock. Are you going to write me a check?

I gotta go home."

It's understandable why New Line Cinema didn't appear in the credits of the remake. At 8:30 the next morning, a rep who hadn't even been at the screening called to pass on the film, making the parking ticket Clay found on his car the night before sting that much more. The studio reps' initial excitement about *Meet the Parents* after the screening is interesting though when one considers that

New Line's initial reluctance to be associated with this low-budget movie had been given as the cause of the death of the National Lampoon distribution deal that had been struck for *Meet the Parents* just the previous year.

Undaunted, Clay then sent faxes to every division of Sony Pictures which had quite a few divisions. Sony International responded and Clay dutifully brought the print over to a screening room which was filled with a bunch of men in suits. The next morning, he received a call stating that the movie wasn't for them. Then, 10 minutes later, another call announced, "We've changed our minds. We liked it! Can we show the print to more people here?"

The print was screened 27 more times. Clay had several meetings with a man named Ted Shugrue, whose office, according to Clay, looked like what one might imagine that of an old-time Hollywood mogul would look like. Not only did he have two assistants, but he also had an outside receptionist and an inside receptionist, a long hallway covered with framed movie posters from past studio triumphs separating the two.

Clay became friendly with the outside receptionist who made him wise to the fact that Shugrue always made people wait 30 minutes from the time of the appointment. After finding this out, Clay would call right before leaving his apartment and ask her to announce him.

That put an end to the half-hour wait time.

Ted seemed interested in the movie but as the receptionist confided to Clay one day, "He can't say 'yes' to everything. Just a little while ago, he said 'no' to James Cameron of all people who wanted to make some movie about a shipwreck."

Of course, Clay would remember this statement vividly in 1997 when James Cameron's *Titanic* was released and went on to rake in $2.195 billion worldwide.

Talks continued and Greg even flew out to meet Shugrue, staying at Clay's place in Marina Del Rey in the meantime. Shugrue was honest about the situation. He told them that there were two ways to go with the movie: The high-octane version with big-name stars, or the low-octane, low-budget version. Movie studios never went for a low-octane version of a movie but new to the business, Greg didn't know that.

Clay and Greg's memories diverge at this point. Clay remembers Shugrue offering $10,000 to option the rights for a few years but they felt it was too low and passed.

Greg can't imagine why they would have said "no" to $10,000 so to the best of his recollection, either Shugrue didn't make an official offer, or he passed on the movie. "Then when the film was about to be sold to Universal," Greg explained, "he made us an offer out of his pocket, but it was something much less than Universal eventually paid."

However it went, Sony International was out of the bidding becoming another in a long line of near misses and not evens.

A showing of the film was arranged at a screening room on Sunset Boulevard and various studio reps attended. As did Weird Al Yankovich, a friend of Emo's, and Dr. Demento, a radio broadcaster who specialized in humorous novelty songs.

Most notable was the rep for Disney, not so much for his presence there then, but for its significance years later. A few years after that meeting, Hollywood Pictures, a film division of Walt Disney Studios, released a third movie starring then-hot comedian Pauly Shore. Son of Mitzi Shore, owner of The Comedy Store, and comedian Sonny Shore, Pauly Shore affected for his act a "surfer dude" demeanor even though he left one questioning whether he'd actually ever seen an ocean. Success for Pauly followed as an MTV VJ and the host of the annual Spring Break specials for the channel.

When the 1992 movie *Encino Man* in which he co-starred with Brendan Fraser turned out to be a hit, Shore went from VJ to movie star, even though each movie seemed to be worse than the one before. A Pauly Shore film was considered far from art and his third film, *Son in Law* released in 1993 was no exception, but it wound up making $36.4 million at the North American box office. The premise is curiously familiar: Shore's character named Crawl goes to meet the family of the girl he's hoping to marry. Of course, fish-out-of-water Crawl makes a mess of it all to what some apparently thought were hilarious results.

The genius of *Meet the Parents* is that the premise is so universal. Other films have used the premise as a foundation. One of the best examples is the 1967 classic *Guess Who's Coming to Dinner* in which the character portrayed by Sidney Poitier goes to meet the very white parents of his very white fiancée (Katharine Houghton), who in turn must meet her fiancée's equally black parents. In that film, the premise was used as a foundation for social commentary. Social convention and a fear of what their kids will face in life is what makes it hard for the parents to Accept their children's choice of mates.

In *Meet the Parents*, Greg Glienna used the premise as a foundation for his subtle dark comedy. There should be no reason for the parents to dislike the character of Greg but for the fact that some cruel trickster god has turned even his most sincere efforts into disasters.

Greg is a victim of circumstance whereas, in *Son in Law*, Shore's character is a victim of his own ineptitude. He has it in his power to create a happy ending and eventually he finds a way to turn the situation around and win the day and his future family's acceptance.

There is no winning for Greg in *Meet the Parents*. Fate has decreed that there will be no happy ending and the family that would have accepted him immediately will instead want to run him out of town. While there are similarities, Shore uses broad humor to tell his story with an ending that owes more to the message of tolerance offered in *Guess Who's Coming to Dinner* than it owes to the sense of discomfort and foreboding found in the dark comedy *Meet the Parents*. We're not laughing because Greg broke the Victrola handle. We're laughing uncomfortably because that should have never happened, yet it did. Because out of all the times that handle has been touched, it chooses to break the moment a young man is trying desperately to impress his future in-laws.

And we have all experienced such a moment.

The interesting thing about this story goes back to the Disney representative who was among other studio representatives at the *Meet the Parents* screening. As Greg explained it, "I heard Pauly Shore on a radio interview actually insisting that the 2000 Universal *Meet the Parents* ripped off *Son in Law* and listing all the similarities. I knew his manager at the time, so I had to call him and tell him to let Pauly know that our original movie came out a few years before his and listing the similarities wasn't really the best idea for him."

Pauly Shore himself was likely unaware of the original *Meet the Parents*. But a Disney rep had been at that screening in 1992, and it was Disney's Hollywood Pictures that produced *Son in Law*. If similarities existed in any of the movies, it would seem Greg and Mary Ruth would have the strongest leg to stand on when bringing up plagiarism.

When *Son in Law* came out its similarities to *Meet the Parents* were not lost on Clay, and he pointed them out to Emo telling the comic that he had proof that Disney had been exposed to *Meet the Parents* before *Son in Law* came out. Emo told him to forget it. When all was said and done, he didn't want to be known as the guy who sued over a Pauly Shore film.

For the screening, however, Clay insisted that Greg and Emo be present so that afterward they "could make deals" out in the hall-way. So, the two flew to LA for a screening that ended up holding about 10 people in the room. Used to seeing the film with a much larger audience and the bigger laughs from them, Greg was uncomfortable by the small number of viewers in the room.

"Emo and I went to wait in the hall to make these 'big deals' but unfortunately, the reps just filed out looking down." Greg and Emo flew back the next day, disappointed but wiser.

A Seminal Movie

Producer Nancy Tenenbaum couldn't believe what she was hearing. Walking away from the assistant she had been talking to, she moved through her New York apartment toward the sound of raucous laughter coming from her living room. There, sitting on the sofa was her brother who'd stopped by to visit, guffawing as he watched the movie she had running in her VCR. She'd been watching it a second time, but then needed to step away to direct her assistant on another project. Her brother's reaction to the film was a revelation. Nancy knew why she liked the movie but was surprised to see a man who was normally drawn to big-budget, splashy comedies react in such a way to a movie with much more subtle humor.

Her brother's reaction was a barometer, and it was a good sign.

Nancy had reached a crossroads, if not in her life, in her way of thinking about the movie business. The movies she'd spent so much effort in helping to put out there, like *Sex, Lies and Video Tape* had achieved levels of success, and had won awards, but it was a success dramatically smaller than other movies with larger budgets.

"*Meet the Parents* came my way right around the time of the independent movie *The Daytrippers*," Nancy explained. "*Daytrippers* was a really funny movie and won all sorts of awards. But honestly, it depressed me that you can work many years on something, and it seems as if it's not seen. I was beginning to feel sour about how no matter how good a movie is, not enough people are seeing it if it's small. I wanted to make movies that reach as many people as possible."

And that meant studio-backed movies with bigger budgets.

Nancy had had many serendipitous moments in her career that aided in her rise in Hollywood. Her first job in the business was as an associate in a joint venture between 20th Century Fox and CBS, prebuying the home video rights to particular properties. At the time, a movie could be financed by prebuying home video rights to English-speaking countries. "I always loved reading and writing," Nancy said, "so I found myself reading literally 30 scripts a week, and I got to know the buyers and the people who had the money as well as producers, directors, actors, and writers."

Frequently the last to leave the office, Nancy was there to take calls from some of the most notable people in the business who called after everyone else had left hoping to just leave a message so a call could be logged, rather than engage with anyone. Getting a live person, rather than an answering machine, at 10:00 at night made them curious as to why she was still there working, and the conversations that ensued enabled her to build relationships with these people. Soon, it led to her role as a producer in such independent features as *The Daytrippers, Mac, The Rapture,* and *Sex, Lies, and Video Tape.*

Another serendipitous moment occurred after she appeared in a panel discussion at a workshop that her friend John Pierson put on. Pierson was the creator and host of *Split Screen,* a television show that ran on the Independent Film Channel from 1997 to 2001 and showcased independent filmmakers in America. He was also instrumental in helping independent filmmakers like Richard Linklater, Spike Lee, Kevin Smith, and Michael Moore get their movies on screen.

"It was very small and intimate," Nancy remembers of the panel. "Maybe fifty people. It was John's first year of trying the workshop."

After the discussion, she was approached by Jim Vincent who had attended the workshop in the hopes of networking. After a quick introduction, he asked if she would be willing to read the script that would later become the movie *A Guy Thing.* Nancy happily agreed and then during the conversation asked if he had done anything else.

"He said, 'Yeah, I produced this movie that we filmed in Chicago with the screenwriter who wrote this script. He wrote, directed, and starred in it. He's a comedian.' I told him I'd love to see it, so he sent me a copy."

The reaction to *Meet the Parents* from both herself and her brother indicated to Nancy that a bigger movie could be made from it. "I saw the movie and thought: This is ridiculous! I can't stop laughing at this thing and it was made for $30,000. What could be done with a bigger budget?"

Reaching out to Greg, Nancy asked if he'd allow her to pitch the movie to people as a possible remake. Since finding a distributor for the original had so far been unsuccessful, Greg agreed. First, she would need financing, but she found herself up against an unexpected roadblock. Sending a copy to a financier she knew overseas, Nancy was surprised by his response "I don't get it." He told her. "It's not funny to me." She gave it to several more who gave her pretty much the same response. She couldn't understand how they were unable to see the potential in such a universal and high-stakes seminal moment in most people's lives. Going home to meet the parents: Nancy thought such a stressful situation was ripe for lots of laughs.

"Maybe people were seeing the movie as smaller than it was, or the concept and possibilities were smaller than they were, and they thought I was looking to do it as a smaller movie. Maybe because I came out of independent film, potential financiers were pegging it as independent."

Nancy stuck with it though. She'd become one of those missionaries that Emo had spoken of. It was almost as if she'd taken up the baton from Clary Heery, the film's previous champion.

Charting a different course, Nancy took it to her friend director Steven Soderberghh with whom she'd had such a good working relationship on *Sex Lies and Videotape* and who would go on to be her producing partner on *The Day Trippers*.

"I remember telling him that I thought this was a seminal movie. 'Everyone goes home to meet their girlfriend's or boyfriend's parents and it's always this incredibly stressful situation. It's a universal theme. It's a huge movie.'"

"As soon as I saw it," Soderbergh remembered, "I said, 'Well this is fantastic!' The problem was my ability at the time to get things going was limited."

Steven Soderbergh graduated high school in 1981 and made his way out to California hoping to get into film making. His first job in the industry was that of a game show composer and cue card holder. But soon he found work editing films freelance. He learned the craft, made contacts and in 1985 was tapped to direct the concert video for the rock group Yes called *9012LIVE* for which he was nominated for a Grammy for Best Music Video Long Form.

When he wrote and directed *Sex, Lies and Video Tape*, starring James Spader and Andie MacDowell and released in 1989, the then 26-year-old director seemed to be starting a most prodigious career. The movie was both critically acclaimed and a success at the box office. Made for $1.2 million, it pulled in $36.7 million worldwide box office, a return on investment that studio executives found very attractive. As a director, Soderbergh had also been the youngest recipient of the Cannes Film Festival's Palme d'Or award.

Everything seemed to be coming up Soderbergh until his next movie, *Kafka* (1991), a biopic about Franz Kafka starring Jeremy Irons. Opening to mixed reviews, it was a flop at the box office, as were his next movies *King of the Hill* (1993), *The Underneath* (1995), and *Schizopolis* (1996).

A lesson taught to the filmmaker Orson Welles, who'd also been considered a prodigy after 1941's *Citizen Kane*, living up to the success of that first big movie can be a difficult thing.

Around the time that Nancy had reached her crossroads regarding the types of films she wanted to make, Steven had begun to question his place in the Hollywood scheme of things. The small independent movies he'd been making just weren't getting the sort of backing or consequently recognition they needed to truly grab a movie audience's attention. And in Hollywood, you're often considered only as good as how well your last movie did at the box office.

So, Steven began casting about for chances to direct movies with larger budgets and themes to help freshen his reputation from that of simply an art-house director.

When Nancy approached him with *Meet the Parents*, a movie itself suffering from the curse of a low budget, Steven saw the potential of it should a major studio back a remake. But his string of flops had taken a little of the sparkle from Hollywood's latest wunderkind and he knew, even with his name attached as director, finding a studio to believe in the film's potential might be a challenge. He had a relationship with Universal though and felt perhaps if he attached himself to the project, he would be able to encourage them to develop it.

With Soderbergh attached as the director, Universal took a vague sort of interest in it (despite its lack of dinosaurs) and the movie went into development. Which often translates into, "We'll get to it when we get to it." Still, they felt enough interest in it to option a screenplay for it and made an offer to Greg and Mary Ruth in November 1994.

Swimming with Sharks

Hollywood: a land of sunshine and dreams. Or so the legend has it. Back before the glitz and glamor, Hollywood was merely a neighborhood centrally located in Los Angeles. Unassuming, undeveloped, ripe for growth. Incorporated in 1903, it joined the city of Los Angeles in 1910, a few years after drawing to it small studios of the burgeoning film industry. When the film industry started, most studios found themselves heading down to Florida to set up shop, attracted by the warmer weather. But that weather could be unpredictable with storms and hurricanes. Hollywood, California offered a more consistent and pleasant climate so studios began to head west. Also attractive for movie makers was that the Wizard of Menlo Park's litigious reach did not seem to extend to California. The U.S.'s first film studio was Black Maria, opened in West Orange, New Jersey by Thomas Edison who had patented the kinetoscope movie viewer that same year. The kinetoscope was actually developed by William Kenney Dickson, one of Edison's assistants, but "who" actually invented a device never stopped Edison when it came to opening a patent on said device. Forming the Motion Picture Patents Company (MPPC) with like-minded patent holders in the new industry, Edison's continual lawsuits against independent filmmakers who crossed his patents made it difficult to operate. Even Florida, to where many of the young movie studios fled, was not far enough away from the Wizard's reach.

But California…moving across the entire country made it hard to enforce rulings favorable to Edison. The name Hollywood, which would become iconic unto itself, was actually inspired by the name of an estate in Illinois when Harvey and Daeida Wilcox appropriated the name to christen the 120-acre ranch they purchased in 1886 near Los Angeles. When the time came for the Wilcox's to downsize, they sold off parcels of land and filmmakers were only too happy to snatch them up, building their studios and an industry at the same time. It wasn't long before the name "Hollywood" became synonymous with that industry.

A movie option can be a curious beast. An agreement between the writer and the studio, it gives the studio a set amount of time to own the rights to make the picture, the movie held in a sort of holding pattern until the studio decides what to do with it, or the option expiration date comes up. In the case of *Meet the Parents*, Universal Pictures had 15 months to essentially cook or get out of the kitchen. Once the option expires, the studio can option the script again, or the writer is free to shop the script around to other studios. Since the writer is paid by the studio every time it renews an option, it's conceivable for a writer to earn a living writing scripts without those movies ever being made.

As one can imagine, Greg and Mary Ruth were thrilled at this turn of events. Finding a distributor for the original film would have been ideal but knowing their creation would be on the big screen again, albeit in the form of a remake, was also exciting. It could also open doors for future work in the industry, depending on how well the film did. And on top of purchasing the option on the movie, Universal offered the pair a writing contract to expand their screenplay into a script for a big-budget film, compensating them well for 12 weeks of writing a "First-Draft Screenplay," six weeks allotted for the "First Rewrite," and three weeks set aside for an optional "Polish" period should that be required.

Even more interesting in the Writing Agreement dated Dec. 5, 1994, there was a clause stating: "If the Picture is produced, and if Writer," [In this case Writer refers to Greg and Mary Ruth] "receives any form of 'Screenplay by' or 'Written by' credit, Universal shall pay Writer the additional sum of $125,000."

Quite a payday considering how they were already being paid a total of $95,000 to write the screenplay (and that's not counting the payment for the option itself). How could they not get "Screenplay" or "Written by" credit on the finished movie when not only had they written the original movie, they had been hired by Universal to write the remake?

Another perk for the pair in the contract could be found in a clause stipulating that, "If Writer receives Sole Screenplay Credit, Writer Shall be entitled to a Right of First Negotiation to Write on the terms set forth in Paragraph 5. of Schedule 1." Which meant that they'd have a chance to negotiate with the studio to write a sequel or remake before any other writer might be considered for the job.

Not a bad deal at all.

The legal departments of movie studios, however, have been drafting movie contracts for over a century and they've gotten very good at constructing what is a legal fortress to protect the assets of the studio. They aren't necessarily looking to cheat the writer, but they also aren't willing to give up any chance they can to cash in as much as they can on the property they're backing.

That's why, per the contract, if Universal exercised their option and made a movie, then,

"Owner hereby sells and assigns to Universal exclusively and forever all motion picture, television, allied and ancillary rights for the entire universe, in any and all languages, in and to the Work, including all of the contents thereof, all the characters therein, all present and future adaptations and revisions thereof and the theme thereof, and in and to the copyright thereof and all renewals and extensions of said copyright (all of the foregoing, hereinafter referred to as the 'Granted Rights'). The Granted Rights shall include, without limitations, the following exclusive and perpetual rights: All Media, Portions, Changes/New, Versions, Copyright, Use of Title, Waiver of Droit Moral, Screenplay/Novelization and Advertising/Publicity Publication, Commercial Tie-ups, Merchandising rights, Theme Park Rights, Broadcasting, Music Publishing Rights, Soundtrack Album Rights, Trademark, Prints and Physical Properties, Derivative Distribution, Personality and Publicity Rights, Other Rights (All other rights of every kind and nature whatsoever)."

That's right. The intellectual property that Greg and Mary Ruth sweated over would become the wholly owned property of Universal, which could pretty much do whatever the studio wished with it as well as put the kibosh on any plans the actual creators might have for it. Even if aliens from another planet, having received transmissions of the movie, were interested in making their version they would be out of luck unless they got the okay from Universal because those rights owned by the studio covered "the entire universe."

As amusing as it is to imagine representatives from Universal in heated negotiations with representatives from Betelgeuse or Tattoine for the "universal" rights to remake *Meet the Parents*, that clause does illustrate just how diligent the effort was to conceive of every possible way the studio could keep the rights to the movie in its grasp. A sort of just-in-case clause. There probably wouldn't be a lot of merchandising involved in a movie like this, but whatever there was, they owned the rights! It's doubtful much thought was given to a commercial soundtrack, but if a soundtrack could be derived from it, BOOM! Universal owned the rights to that.

Again, Hollywood movie studios have had decades to imagine the possibilities and when it came to rights, they're ready to establish them for any possibility.

It is a bitter pill that for decades screen writers, perhaps more than writers in any other industry, have had to swallow because from page to screen, making a movie is such a collaborative process. Directors, unit directors, producers, editors, cinematographers, and studio heads, all have a say, for good and for ill, in the way the story is told. Some writers look upon a studio contract as a deal with the devil: writers have the choice to become independents by funding their own films, as Greg and many others started to do around that time, but scaring up the funds to do it justice, can be a battle in itself. Orson Welles, one of the original indie filmmakers, farmed himself to other productions to raise the money to make the films he wanted to make in his way. Unfortunately, lack of funds often left his productions lagging for months, sometimes years before they were complete.

There was also the added cost of finding distribution for the film, as Greg found out with his original film. The alternative is to sign the script over to a studio that has the resources for a big budget and cross your fingers that the decisions of all those people handling it won't make the film stray too far from your creative vision.

Director Quentin Tarantino made such a compromise when he sold the script for *Natural Born Killers* to producers Jane Hamsher and Don Murphy to get the money to fund the production of his 1992 debut film *Reservoir Dogs*. Starring Woody Harrelson and Juliette Lewis, *Natural Born Killers* raised a lot of controversy at the time for its violence, but on a budget of $35 million it took in $110 million at the box office. Tarantino, who had tried to film his own version of *Killers* but was unable to raise the funding, sold it to the two producers who in turn sold it to Warner Bros. From there it fell into the hands of director Oliver Stone who rewrote it with Richard Rutkowski and David Veloz, changing the whole tone of Tarantino's original vision. The version that hit the screen had deviated so much from Tarantino's original script that he received only "Story" credit, a credit he eventually demanded be taken off the movie because he was so unhappy with the final release.

After screenwriter Paul Rudnick's script for *Sister Act* was pitched to producer Scott Rudin, Disney bought it with an eye toward Bette Midler in the lead. When Midler turned it down, Whoopi Goldberg signed on and the script went into development. Along the way, six writers got involved with the script, changing it to the point where the script was nothing like Rudnick's original work. Unhappy with the result, but not enough to give up the money a screenwriting credit would bring, Rudnick kept the credit under the pseudonym Joseph Howard. *Sister Act* was released in May 1992 and pulled in $231.6 million at the box office on a $31 million budget, so the changes apparently didn't harm the movie.

Unless a screenwriter has the clout to negotiate a contract more in their favor (and most do not), then they'll end up having to risk compromising their vision a little to get it out there.

With no one else beating down the door for *Meet the Parents*, Greg knew this was the movie's best shot to be noticed.

One contractual stipulation did concern him. All rights to the 1992 film would belong to Universal, which insisted on calling it a "short" because of its 76-minute run time. Thus, Greg would have to obtain permission from Universal before the original could be shown for any reason. What ultimately ended up happening was that Greg's *Meet the Parents* was locked up in a contractual vault and allowed to slowly evaporate from memory while the studio took its sweet time getting a remake done.

For over a century, films have been remade. The 1937 film *A Star is Born* has been remade three times and will probably be remade for another generation eventually. Some films are remade for better, some for worse. And once video players came about, leading to DVD, Blu-ray, and streaming, people have been able to access more originals and remakes without a problem. Rarely, however, does one hear about the original being buried somewhere in a legal vault of the studio producing the remake.

In the decades since that contract with Universal was signed though, the original *Meet the Parents* has rarely been shown outside of a few film festivals because Universal is so cagey about allowing it to be viewed.

It was a clause, perhaps that should have been better negotiated at the time of signing.

Opportunities like this for new writers are so special though, it's understandable that people might not want to tempt fate by demanding too much for fear that the company they're doing business with might take offense and take away the opportunity. So, they sign, hoping that the working relationship will be such that the company would never deny so simple a request.

And Greg and Mary Ruth were writing the script for the remake, so the world would know that they were the ones behind *Meet the Parents*. What could go wrong?

Reworking the Script

Greg and Mary Ruth were flown to New York to work on a script for the *Meet the Parents* remake. Over the next few days, they met with both Nancy and Steven Soderbergh to discuss additions and omissions from their original screenplay, then they met with a representative from Universal to whom Soderbergh gave what Greg terms, "A dazzling pitch of the movie."

The basic premise worked well as did many of the gags, but the movie itself needed to be expanded upon, a definite third act arrived at. And Nancy was anxious to convince the fledgling screenwriters to ditch the wrap-around scenes of the gas station attendant and his cautionary tale and go with a straighter narrative. One thing troubling the original 1992 movie was simply its low budget. There was a claustrophobic feeling to it since it was written with few locations to keep the cost of filming low. There are scenes in the original where it's apparent that the production's financial limitations kept it from where it could have gone with some of the gags. For example, in the scene where Greg offers to go to the drug store and Mr. Burns insists that the young man use his car, tossing him the keys. In the film, the character of Greg manages to damage the car's passenger side mirror in the store parking lot and winds up later being hit at an intersection by an oncoming car running a stop sign. Both instances help to set up Greg's weekend from hell, but it's that deliciously nervous ride up to that point that holds the most satisfaction for the audience. With a bigger budget, more could have been done to lengthen that tension before the car is damaged. "That's something I wanted to do," Greg said. "I wanted it to be a big sequence with all these near misses. Have a ball roll out into the street with kids chasing it into the path of the car. Have a fire engine getting behind him honking. That could have been a classic scene. He gets a fire engine riding on his bumper and he's gotta do 90 miles an hour in Dad's car. Then some little old lady crosses the street. It could be a whole near-miss of things he almost hit that could have played out for ten minutes. But we couldn't do it for $30,000."

With a major studio's backing, Greg and Mary Ruth could be much more creative with the predicaments they put their hapless protagonist in.

Also needed was a third act which the original movie didn't have. At least for the main story. The wrap-around scenes for the 1992 movie were those filmed in the gas stating leading off and ending it. It was a straightforward horror story with no concern for character arcs. The conclusion of the main story itself was left up to the audience's imagination as a father frustrated out of his mind is seen cocking a rifle at the top of the stairs and Greg is seen looking up the stairs at him like a deer in the headlights.

Fade to black and back to the gas station where the attendant tells another horror story about circuses to a different guy taking his family to one.

In the script that Greg and Mary Ruth wrote for Universal, the gas station bit was abandoned, and a much more typically structured story was created including something they originally didn't have: a true reconciliation moment for Greg. The 1992 *Meet the Parents* had a forgiveness moment when the family is in church and taking to heart the priest's homily of forgiveness which encourages them to forgive Greg. This just leads to a false relaxation of tension before the horror of the tale ends as fate trips Greg up once again.

In a Hollywood movie, there would need to be that moment where the cast, having ridden through their dark night of the soul, now reaches their happily ever after. Universal would want a movie where the audience got their warm and fuzzy conclusion and Greg and Mary Ruth tried their best to deliver that.

In early 1995 they delivered a new, extended first draft based on their original screenplay, followed by a second draft a few months later. The project retained the title *Meet the Parents* and was placed on Universal's list of "maybe one-day" projects. Not an unusual status in Hollywood. In the meantime, Nancy did her best to keep the project from plunging into "development hell": the unique journey some movie projects embark upon as studios try to figure out what to do with them while not wanting to give up the option to them. Even if the project doesn't leave the studio, it can often go through directors, producers, and writers for years before a finished product hits the screens. If a finished product comes out of it.

It's not unusual for a script to pass through the hands of several writers before a final shooting script is decided upon. Sometimes this is a good thing. New pairs of eyes bringing in fresh ideas can complement a script.

Yet sometimes writing by committee can lead to fragmentation of the whole. Greg would experience this with another script he sold while *Meet the Parents* was nearing production.

A Guy Thing came out of the idea he'd been carrying around for years where a man's infidelity is discovered after he wins a lottery. The lottery idea was ditched, and the infidelity story was expanded upon. What Greg came away with was a script he felt proud to shop around. Bought by MGM in 1999 it was put into production as a vehicle for Jason Lee and Julia Stiles. And that's where the problems began. Greg watched helplessly as his tight and polished script was edited and changed by a series of script doctors brought in to please various factions in the production.

"Charlie Chaplin once said one of the hardest things in comedy is sustaining your enthusiasm," Greg stated. "First, they're like, 'Oh it's in great shape. Just get rid of this dark ending.' Then I turn in the next draft, and they read it again and again and again. 'Well, why don't you look at the dialogue here? Maybe it can be funnier.' Then they get rewriters, and they print jokey, jokey, jokey. And then they get a cast and Julia Stiles has ideas and the cast has ideas. She wanted a female writer, so they got a female writer to do what Julia Stiles wanted. By the time it came out it was just a mishmash."

Critics noted this as well. Dennis Harvey from Variety stated in his Jan. 15, 2003 review of the movie, "Though… 'A Guy Thing' does get slightly better as it goes along, the presence of four (credited) scenarists suggests a familiar syndrome at play: Whatever creative spark or individuality might have existed in early drafts got 'polished' into oblivion between rewrites."

While Paul Clinton of CNN in his Jan. 17, 2003 review of A Guy Thing pointed out, "The script is a perfect example of too many chefs spoiling the broth…Something horrible definitely happened between the pitch session and the final product."

"By the time that script sold," Greg remembered, "it was a perfect script. It was a farce that started off running and just built and built and built. My entertainment lawyer said it was the funniest script he'd ever read. And they just killed it. I remember at the premiere, these two guys who were the other writers who came aboard later, came up to me and said, 'All the laughs were yours.' The only thing that got laughs was the stuff they left alone."

There was little he could do. Greg had sold the script to MGM, and they could do what they wished with the movie. Once the contracts are signed, it becomes the studio's property. That is the way of things in Hollywood. He would of course receive residuals, but it would not be for a movie he was proud of. A Guy Thing opened on Jan. 17, 2003, to a weak box office and fell from sight not long after that.

Of course, by that point, Greg had already experienced the fickleness of Hollywood, his experience with the remake of Meet the Parents being his first dose of cold water.

PHOTOS

Dick Galloway and Carol Whelan as Irv and Kay Burns

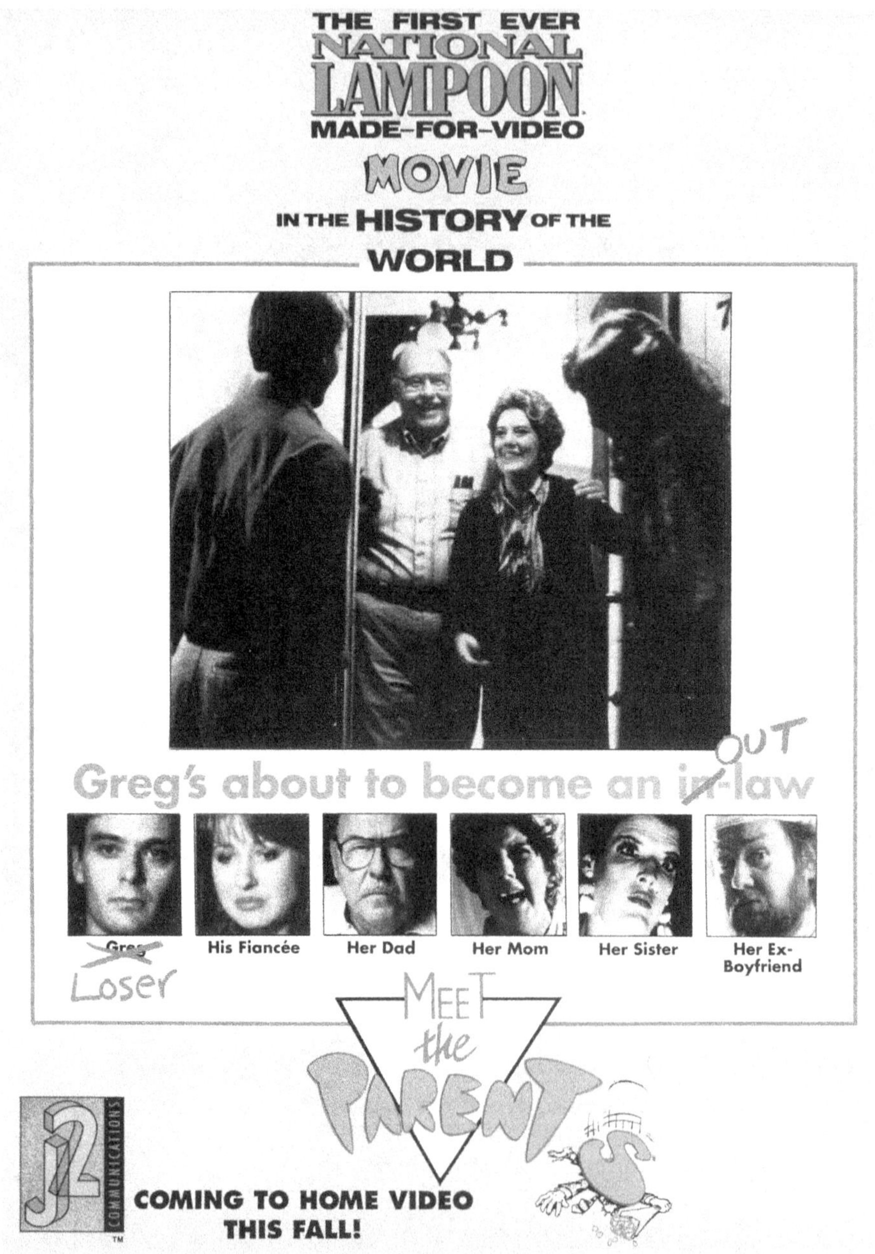

Ad From National Lampoon Announcing
The Home Video Debut Of Meet the Parents.

Emo Philips As The Video Store Clerk Recommending Titles
To Greg For Family Viewing Night

Greg Glienna

Newspaper Ad For One Of Greg's Early Comedy Gigs

Mary Ruth Clarke

"enormously funny. . .a very funny, very original piece of work"
Dave Kerr
Chicago Tribune

"extremely bizarre and funny"
Peter Sobczynski
The Chicago Flame

"Hilarious"
Ted Shen
Chicago Reader

"very funny, very strange. I loved it'
Norman Mark
WMAQ-TV

"very funny sight gags"
John Petrakis
New City

"a highly original nightmare comedy"
Kevin Sweeny
Skyline

"genuinely funny"
Ernest Tucker
Chicago Sun Times

**FRIDAYS & SATURDAYS AT MIDNIGHT
thru MAY 2nd**

Handout for Meet The Parents Showing At The Music Box Theatre

Poster For Meet The Parents Created By National Lampoon

Awards Presented to Glienna's 2023 Independent Film *The Road Dog*

Poster For Glienna's Independent Movie *The Road Dog*

Chicago's Historic Music Box Theatre

Mike Toomey

The Log Cabin Bar In Des Plaines

The Original Meet the Parents Was Shown For A Week in
September 2024 At The Pickwick Theatre In Park Ridge

Establishing his Narrative

After Greg and Mary Ruth submitted their second draft, it was felt by Kevin Misher, a new production executive joining Universal fresh from a six-year tenure at Tri-Star Pictures, that a writer with more experience in the industry would be needed to take their *Meet the Parents* script to the next level. Nancy kept pitching writer after writer she felt would work well with the tone they were trying to set for the film but each one was rejected, until, according to Nancy, "Eventually we kind of settled on Jim Herzfeld."

A 1984 graduate of the UCLA School of Theater, Film, and Television, Jim Herzfeld had not racked up many movie credits by the time *Meet the Parents* came along. His first gig was writing for the first season of *It's Garry Shandling's Show* in 1986 though as he remembers it, "My credit on that is 'researcher' because I wasn't in the Writers Guild," and for the series to have him back under the status of writer, he would need to write a feature film to join the guild. Later he worked as a producer on *The Trouble with Larry, Married…With Children,* and *Doctor Doctor.*

His first foray into the land of movies was with a "Story" credit on the 1988 cult classic *Tapeheads* starring John Cusack and Tim Robbins. But as he explains it, he and his friend Ryan Rowe, who co-wrote the movie with him, deserved a much larger credit than that. "The producer and director took a run through our draft and said, 'Oh we're taking Screenplay credit.' If you looked at my early drafts and you looked at the movie you'd be like, 'They used a ton of your stuff. How come you didn't get Screenplay?' Because I wasn't in the Writers Guild. And they offered me and my friend Ryan…you know we were just out of college and broke as fuck and they said, 'We'll give you $3,000 each if you take your name off Screenplay.' And we went, 'Boy we're getting boned here but okay, we'll take it!

You know I'm going to use that money to buy my first-word processor.'"

His was a pragmatic response that would serve him well in dealing with the fickleness of the writing credit process. It's also a particularly ironic story when one considers the way the screen credits would play out for the 2000 *Meet the Parents*.

While later he would be credited with "Screenplay" for *Meet the Deedles* and was credited with "Teleplay" on *Jungle Book: Mowgli's Story*, *Meet the Parents* would turn out to be the biggest movie he'd worked on by that point.

In 1996, Herzfeld was approached to help with the script and initially, according to Nancy, she and Jim got along well. But here's where the story becomes particularly convoluted as both seem to have two completely different memories of how Jim came aboard and how things progressed from there.

According to Nancy, it was after he'd inked the deal with Universal that Herzfeld told them he wouldn't be able to work on the script for several months because he had to work on another script. "I was really bummed out. You know it was just another annoying thing [in this process]," Nancy explained. "He probably knew we wouldn't have gone with him if we knew he wouldn't be available to work on it. This would mean he wouldn't start till September, October, November. Something like that."

Universal went through several regimes from 1994-2000, which added to the delay in development. With every new regime, Nancy had to build enthusiasm for the movie all over again, convincing the new bosses that *Meet the Parents* was a property well worth the investment. Every little step was progress, but it was slow going and Nancy knew she was racing against time. Steven Soderbergh was still on board to direct, but he couldn't wait forever. He was looking to change his fortunes and would need to take on a project soon. Both Nancy and Greg believed that as a director, Steven would best be able to give the movie the finesse that was right for it. If the project lost him, they weren't sure what would come of it.

For Universal, the project just wasn't that important. It was important enough to renew options on the script but not a whole lot of effort was expended after that.

"Remember," Nancy explained, "This wasn't a project they believed in. I remember talking to Kevin Misher and saying, 'Jim's not going to be able to start till…' whenever and Kevin saying, 'Aw, that's okay.' Looking back on it I see because they weren't that excited about it, they were in no rush. And let's face it they have hundreds of projects in development, this wasn't a priority at this point."

It is curious that a writer would take on a project with one studio and tell them that he wouldn't be able to begin until he finished a project with another studio. But it depends on what was in Herzfeld's contract and what allowances Universal made. If they were on the fence about making the movie, then they might have contractually allowed him the leeway to finish the one project before officially starting his *Meet the Parents* draft.

From what Greg remembers of that time, the script that Herzfeld left to work on was the 1998 movie *Meet the Deedles*. "I never saw it, but I guess I named that movie too because he changed the title to *Meet the Deedles* after he started working on our script. Originally it was *The Deedles* and then it became *Meet the Deedles*."

Considering how Deedles rhymes with Beatles, the title could have been a play on words of the title from the iconic group's first U.S.-released album *Meet the Beatles* chosen by the execs at Disney when they optioned the movie.

Or it could have been Herzfeld cashing in on a title that he was realizing had a lot of potential. Whatever the inspiration for the title, the film was anything but inspired. Released by Disney, the movie was a *Dumb and Dumber* wanna-be featuring surfer dudes that was four years too late to ride the wave of the goofball duo trend that was already dying out. Think *Bill and Ted* or *Wayne's World* without the sweetness, cleverness, or likability. The critics were not kind and the movie grossed only $4.4 million of its $24 million budget. The movie has since gone out of print. Though it is accessible on Disney + streaming.

In a 2017 panel discussion held by the Writer's Guild of America, and available on YouTube, Herzfeld explained that his first spec script was a movie called *The Deedles, Down on the Farm* written in 1987 which was vastly different than the movie released by Disney a decade later. "National Lampoon optioned it," he told the audience. "And we were actually going to preproduction and scouting locations on it when it turned out that the guy who was running Lampoon at the time, who was like Hollywood's version of Bernie Madoff I think…he seemed to have all this money and then suddenly he was on the lam and Interpol was looking for him and…I don't know."

And so that film was never made.

Researching Lampoon's history, there doesn't seem to be any names involved around the time that Herzfeld indicates his script was optioned by the company that scream "embezzlement", especially embezzlement so severe that Interpol or any similar organization got involved. Certainly, nothing that stopped the film division from cranking out movies. Two movies in the *Vacation* series, *European Vacation* and *Christmas Vacation* were released in 1985 and 1989 respectively, bookending the period that Herzfeld implied locations for his *Deedles* movie were being scouted. While there does seem to be four years between *Christmas Vacation* and the 1993 release of *Loaded Weapon 1*, that could be due to a reorganization after the brand was taken over by Jim Jimirro and J2 Communications. And the films began to again crank out in 1994.

Years later, the closest case even matching Herzfeld's description involved Dan Laikin who, with Timothy Durham and several other Indiana-based investors, began to buy up shares of J2 Communications, Inc. Once they acquired a majority share in the company,

Laikin's consortium began concentrating on bringing the National Lampoon brand back to its former glory. Similar to the vision that Jim Jimirro had for the brand in the 1990s, the company that became National Lampoon, Incorporated under Laikin, Durham, and their co-investors delved into a variety of media business, from movies to TV, to print, and even the "largest Internet-based comedy network in the world."

That was in 2001 though. By 2010, Laikin was sentenced to 45 months in prison for conspiring to inflate the company's stock price. A few years after that, Timothy Durham, who had taken over as CEO of National Lampoon, was convicted of 10 counts of fraud, one count of securities fraud, and one count of conspiracy as a result of a scheme to defraud investors of $200 million in the Ohio-based investment business Fair Finance Company.

While it was uncertain if Interpol was involved, The FBI and the SEC (Securities and Exchange Commission) were both involved in the cases. But the cases happened well after *Meet the Parents* came out, let alone *Meet the Deedles*, and should have had no bearing what-so-ever on National Lampoon finishing the movie Jim Herzfeld says they optioned from him.

So, it is curious (and quite coincidental) that, a company at the time trying to build its movie brand, would ditch a movie they were preparing to film, even down to scouting locations, but as Greg himself experienced when they offered to distribute his *Meet the Parents* on video, it wasn't unusual for Lampoon to back out of deals even after the contracts had been signed.

Still, Herzfeld didn't lose out completely, cashing the check from Disney a decade later even though they had altered his original script into what he termed, "...a piece of crap by Disney called *Meet the Deedles*."

If, as Greg remembers, this was the movie that Herzfeld decided to temporarily ditch *Meet the Parents* for, it was an interesting move, especially given his dislike for the resulting *Deedles* movie.

"After we found out that he wouldn't be able to start on the movie," Nancy stated, "I told him, 'Well if that's the case then we have to beat the whole thing out now so when you start writing in the fall, you are ready to go.' I wanted a road map for the movie, he agreed, and we beat out the movie. I then submitted a 15-page beat sheet to the studio because I was really trying to push the process so that literally, when he came back from his other writing gig, he could start immediately."

Jim Herzfeld's recollections of that time differ dramatically from those of Nancy Tenenbaum, who he stated a few times in an interview for this book that he never met. In fact, according to what he remembers, his involvement with the script was a much less collaborative process than Nancy indicated and doesn't seem to have a lot to do with Universal for that matter.

According to Herzfeld, his involvement with the film came about after Paul Haas from Creative Artists Agency (CAA) sent him a copy of a short film, telling him, "Universal owns this film and they think there might be a movie in it. Why don't you look at it and see what you would do?" It was the 1992 *Meet the Parents*. In Herzfeld's story, he sat on the couch with a legal pad, watching the movie, deciding which bits to keep which needed a little tweaking. He felt the concept was simple yet good, but the execution of the story needed to be different. In the original movie, there isn't much of a reason given for why Greg and Pam are traveling to the home of her parents. It seems to be simply a weekend visit that conveniently enough enables Pam to introduce Greg to her parents for the first time.

Jim felt there needed to be a larger reason for the pair to make the trip and he thought Greg and Pam going back home to attend Pam's sister's wedding and Greg deciding to take the opportunity to ask Pam's father for her hand in marriage might just be what was needed. This opened him up to other ideas and he wrote a draft. He seemed certain that Greg wanting to propose was unique to his draft. In fact, his original idea was to have the proposal occur in the stands of Wrigley Field during a baseball game but was told the budget wouldn't allow for it.

While he may think the proposal was unique to him, a proposal does appear in the drafts that Greg and Mary Ruth wrote for Universal before he came on board, the original idea being that Greg would attempt to propose to Pam while they dined in a Chinese restaurant, the romantic message delivered to her in a fortune cookie. And eventually, in that draft, Greg is encouraged to hold off on the proposal until he can ask Pam's father for his blessing. (Coincidentally enough, according to Nancy, in one of the drafts written by Greg and Mary Ruth, there was also a scene set in Wrigley Field similar to the scene with the gas station attendant in the original movie whereas they watch the game, one fan in the stands tells another the cautionary tale of a man going to meet his girlfriend's parents).

And while Jim Herzfeld seems to remember bringing up the character of Greg needing to ask Pam's father for her hand, Nancy indicates it was in the drafts written by Greg and Mary Ruth. "That was my big thing," she indicated. "I knew this because my husband had just gone to my father's house to ask for my hand in marriage, which was kind of archaic in my mind, so I was thinking of getting into that."

According to Herzfeld, one of the things drawing him to get involved with the project was that Steven Soderbergh was attached as director. "He only had a couple of films under his belt at that point, but he didn't typically make bad films," Herzfeld commented.

"I met with him a couple of times just to run treatments of the movie kind of like, 'Here's what I'm thinking' and honestly, I don't know anything that he said to me that made me go in a different direction but at least he was kind of chuckling and would go, 'Yeah that sounds good.' 'Yeah, go with that.' So that was encouraging."

In Herzfeld's mind, perhaps because of Soderbergh's involvement, *Meet the Parents* was going to be similar in scope to Soderbergh's previous, smaller movies. "I was always thinking this was gonna be back in the day kind of a lower budget little film. You know, Soderbergh. Maybe get John Cusack to play Greg. It'll be a funny, little quirky comedy that people in urban cities will like. It wouldn't necessarily be a blockbuster."

This observation, of course, flies in the face of what Nancy and Soderbergh's stated expectations were. They were looking for big movies to be involved with and Nancy spent a couple of years trying to convince Universal how big *Meet the Parents* could be.

Yet according to Herzfeld, when the director read his first draft, Soderbergh told Jim, "This is really great and it's way too commercial for me." And bowed out after that.

"That's almost a direct quote," Jim said. "No surprise, I worked in television and everything. I have a commercial sensibility. So, I was a little like, oh that's a bummer. So, I wasn't like, oh my god, we lost Soderbergh, this is gonna go nowhere now. I was like, let's see where this goes."

Herzfeld seems to imply that Soderbergh was chased off by the commercial nature of his script. As Nancy tells it, it wasn't the commercial nature of Herzfeld's script that chased Soderbergh off, but rather, how long it took the writer to get a finished script to them. In an interview with the Website "Ain't it Cool News," Herzfeld stated that he finished his draft "five or six months later [after starting] and... big surprise...nothing happened." Again, as Nancy remembered, Herzfeld wouldn't start the first draft until after he finished another project, which took a considerable amount of time. Six or seven months after that could mean that it took nearly a year and a half before his draft of *Meet the Parents* was finished.

"When Jim really went to write and gave me what he thought was the finished draft," Nancy explained, "I said to him, 'Let's change some of this because Greg was very unsympathetic in his draft.' I didn't want to follow a very unlikable character."

When she pointed this out to Kevin Misher, he agreed, saying, "No, he's not likable. Let's go for another draft. Let's tweak it a bit."

"Having been through this with Universal for years," she said, "I wanted it to be right before I submitted it to them because I was afraid, they would pass again, and then it would be in a sort of turn around thing."

According to Nancy, Herzfeld took the notes she had regarding this draft and went back to work on the issues pointed out. The next draft he offered her, though, didn't seem to address the main concern.

"It was still feeling heartless," she said. "The character was kind of nasty and kind of an ass. I said, 'Jim, you know we have to make him nicer. You have to be able to relate to him. And sympathize with him.' And he said, 'No, that's all I'm doing. I'm not doing any more writing. That's it.' I handed it to Kevin and Kevin came back and said, 'You know he's not the most likable character.' I said, 'Yeah, I know. Jim won't do any more writing unless we pay him.'"

Even if the six months Jim states it took him to finish the first draft started from the moment he watched the original movie, when you factor in a couple of times, he was asked to work on the character of Greg, there was still quite a delay. In the interview for this book, Herzfeld did not indicate that he was ever asked to tweak anything with his script. His lack of detail in those months or years (depending on who you believe) of the writing process implies that he hit the ground running with his script. While he contended that his script gave Soderbergh pause over its commerciality, "Other people were saying, 'Hey you did a great job on the script.'"

Nancy on the other hand explained that her main concern was that the long delay in firming up the script would cost them Soderbergh.

Which ultimately it did.

As early as February 1997, Soderbergh was being eyed for the chance to direct the movie *Out of Sight*, starring George Clooney and Jennifer Lopez. When finally, he was offered the job, he could not turn it down. Released in June of 1998, the movie would become a critical and box-office success and help Clooney make a full transition to a bona fide movie star as well as start Soderbergh on a new path as a genre director of box office hits. Soderbergh would go on to direct *Erin Brockovich, Traffic,* and the hit *Ocean* franchise to name a few movies, all successful with critics and the public.

Soderbergh's choice of *Out of Sight* would seem to belie Herzfeld's claim that he was nervous about how commercial Herzfeld's *Meet the Parents* script was and fit with Nancy's narrative that the director was looking to direct bigger movies. It is possible that Soderbergh's reputation and perhaps an initial concern about Herzfeld's script gave the writer the impression that Soderbergh didn't feel prepared for a commercial venture. It's possible too that there were elements in Herzfeld's script that the director felt would be better toned down a little. It's also possible that Herzfeld, believing his script was good to go as is mistook such comments for Soderbergh's doubts about whether he could direct such a big movie successfully.

Whatever pulled Soderbergh away from the project, he was gone, and Nancy couldn't help but wonder if she and Universal shared the same vision of what the movie could be. Nevertheless, she soldiered on, trying to guide the project as best as she could.

Nancy remembers sending the script to David O. Russell, who had made a name for himself with films like *Flirting with Disaster* and *Three Kings,* thinking he might have the finesse required to direct *Meet the Parents.* She even suggested Ben Stiller might be a good fit to direct. Definitely to star in it. Other directors were being considered but none seemed right for the project. "In 1988, I went and saw Ben's standup act, so we were all really young," Nancy stated. "Like I remember it to this day. And I got in touch with him. I remember we were kicking around New York and started talking about things we wanted to do and working together. He ended up getting his *Ben Stiller Show* on MTV like a few weeks later."

Stiller showed her some of his short films, which impressed her, and over the years his skills as a director blossomed. "He's really talented. He likes to get it right as a director." She felt he had the "everyman" relatability needed to play the character of Greg and would be able to bring that sense to the movie as a director. When directors were being considered for *Meet the Parents*, Nancy suggested Stiller feeling he would have just the right touch.

On June 14, 1996, the comedy, *The Cable Guy* was released to theaters. Directed by Stiller, the film is notable for many things, one of them being star Jim Carrey's salary. With that movie, Jim Carrey became the first actor to be paid $20 million to star in a film. It wasn't a huge surprise considering his meteoric success after his stint in *The Mask*. The film, however, opened to mixed reviews and while it made $55 million more than its budget of $47 million, it didn't reach the number expected for a Jim Carrey film at the time. To be fair, however, many went into the movie expecting another wacky Carrey film and were greeted with a much darker comedy.

Whether it was the reception of *The Cable Guy* or Stiller's lack of experience with directing major motion pictures, Universal turned down Nancy's suggestion of hiring Ben Stiller to direct *Meet the Parents*, leaving the hunt for a director back at square one.

Then, Kevin Misher suggested that Nancy go to see a movie that just opened and was getting quite a lot of buzz. It was 1997 and Nancy was getting nervous at how long developing *Meet the Parents* was dragging on, as well as the tapdancing she had to do to keep the studio interested. They needed to find a director to help push this forward and she could only hope that one would be found before the studio again cast its gaze to other projects and away from *Meet the Parents*.

Games People Play

Every so often a movie comes along that takes people by surprise. *Austin Powers: International Man of Mystery* was just such a movie. Very little pre-release buzz heralded this spoof of 1960s spy films starring Mike Meyers and Elizabeth Hurley, but the movie ended up becoming wildly successful. It grossed $67.7 million worldwide, on a $16.5 million budget spawning two sequels and a hell of a lot of catch phrases.

At the helm of this movie was a director by the name of Jay Roach whose first feature film, *Zoo Radio,* had been released in 1990. As a director, he didn't have a lot of films under his belt when Kevin Misher suggested that Nancy check out his latest, *Austin Powers.* *Austin Powers* was only the second film that Roach had directed.

There is some question as to exactly how Jay Roach's name came into play as a possible director for *Meet the Parents.* According to his interview with Ain't it Cool News, Jim Herzfeld took credit for getting the script to Roach. "So, for a few months, the script just sat there, until my agents slipped it to a 'hot, new director' named Jay Roach. Jay was just coming off his first film (a lil' sleeper called AUSTIN POWERS) and he'd read MTP and wanted it to be his next film. Jay and I met, hit it off, and then Jay had a meeting where he all but begged Universal to let him direct it."

In the interview for this book, Jim elaborated on the more circuitous route it took to get to Roach, stating that once he had finished the draft, he showed it to Paul Haas whose reaction was, "This is great but I'm really more a TV guy. So, I'm going to send it to six people in features and see what they think." After a weekend read where it went out to five or six people, Todd Feldman, a features guy at CAA contacted him and told him, "I'm reading your script and it's amazing! I really want to shop this and work it."

A curious development considering that this was a script that Herzfeld was hired to write for a movie already under option at a major studio. For their part, Nancy and Universal had no idea that any of this was going on though according to Nancy, "We asked for another rewrite and then we heard Jim had given it to Jay and he said he didn't think any changes needed to be made. He liked the characters as they were. And that was my reason for not thinking Jay was the right guy to direct. For me, rooting for and liking the main character going through the horrendous weekend is what I believe is essential to its success."

Be that as it may, according to Herzfeld, quickly after the script was being "shopped around," it wound up in the hands of Jay Roach, fresh from *Austin Powers* who was looking for his next project. "He read my draft," Herzfeld stated, "and said, 'Oh I want this to be my next movie.'"

He contacted Jim and asked for a meeting, driving out to Herzfeld's house for a discussion in the backyard. "We talked about what he would do. I don't remember specifics too much. But he was enthusiastic and had some momentum and I was like, 'Oh, I hope this works out.'"

Universal's response? "They liked the script, but they were not nearly as convinced this was as much a project to greenlight as a lot of other people around me, so they kind of shut it down a bit." Universal, according to Herzfeld, was not ready to say yes to Jay Roach.

Which tracks with Nancy's recollections.

Kevin Misher suggested to Nancy that she check out Roach's new film (possibly upon Herzfeld's suggestion), but Misher himself wasn't overly enthusiastic about Roach either. He approached her, saying, "I don't know. He's being recommended to me. Take a look at *Austin Powers*. Let me know what you think."

After watching *Austin Powers*, Nancy was not completely sold on the idea of Roach as a director for *Meet the Parents*, although later she would admit that could have partly been due to the stress, she'd been under simply trying to keep *Meet the Parents* from falling through the cracks. "I went to see *Austin Powers* with the eye that Kevin Misher was going to pass on it. Cause he said, 'Go see this movie, I don't think it's very good but tell me what you think.' I think I went in to see the movie already dejected, thinking, 'Oh my God! Why am I going to see this if this is going to be an uphill battle with this guy?' I actually liked *Austin Powers,* more seeing it again later when I wasn't under pressure and thinking that Roach might either seal the deal or kill the deal. Is this gonna help me get the movie made? It had been such a struggle in keeping them interested, and if they're not going to be interested in him, then am I going to spend another three years not getting the movie made?"

It seemed the higher-ups at Universal had their own concerns when Roach's name was pitched for the movie, despite the success of *Austin Powers*, and they eventually said "no" to the choice.

Roach, however, really wanted a chance at the movie. "The project appealed to me right away," he stated in a March 2001 Barnes & Noble interview. "I liked the script from the beginning, although I felt it needed more work." When the opportunity to direct the film *Mystery, Alaska* came up, Roach jumped at the chance though his eagerness to do that film may have carried an ulterior motive.

As Greg explained it, "Jay Roach told me that *Mystery, Alaska* was sort of an audition to show Universal that he could direct a more down-to-earth film."

Set in the fictional town of the same name, the film details an amateur hockey team preparing for an exhibition game against The New York Rangers. For an audition, it didn't seem to perform very well. With a budget of $28 million, it grossed only $8,891,623 and received mixed reviews. Its humor, however, was lower key than *Austin Powers* so there was some indication that Roach could handle a movie with a premise that was more down to earth. Therefore, while the movie wasn't a hit, the quality of the direction in *Mystery, Alaska,* made Universal give Jay Roach a second look.

Meanwhile, as the hunt for a director was going on in LA, Greg Glienna awoke one day in Chicago to a curious headline in one of the Hollywood periodicals he'd been subscribing to. "It was in Variety or the Hollywood Reporter. I can't remember which," he related, "but the headline was something like 'Jim Carrey eyeing Herzfeld's *Meet the Parents.*'"

It was a surprise for Greg. First because if anything it should read "Universal's *Meet the Parents*" since the script had been in development at the studio long before Herzfeld came on the scene and he'd only been brought on to help take it to the next level.

But also, because the last thing Greg had heard was that Steven Soderbergh was still attached to direct. According to this article, though, Steven Spielberg was considering directing.

Spielberg's name being attached to the project equally confounded Nancy who knew that the delay in the project had lost Soderbergh, but had no idea how DreamWorks, Spielberg, or Carrey got a hold of the script since no one she knew at Universal had sent them a copy.

In a December 2020 interview Roach did for Yahoo News, he took the credit, stating that, "I wasn't able to convince people to let me do it and, in the meantime, I sent it to somebody at Spielberg's company." That would have been DreamWorks Pictures, the studio founded by Spielberg, Jeffery Katzenberg, and David Geffen in 1994.

It seems odd that a director, so hungry for a particular project, would willingly offer up said project to another director. Especially since that project was not his to offer up to anybody's company.

There was another, and perhaps a more likely candidate for who slipped the script to Spielberg & Co., and for many years, Nancy had a theory on who it might have been.

"I think what happened was Jim Herzfeld was very offended that we asked him to go back and do some rewrites and I think his managers probably sent it out there. And one of the people I would imagine they sent it to was maybe Jim Carrey. Maybe Spielberg. The article referring to it as 'Jim Herzfeld's *Meet the Parents*' makes me think that it was definitely from his managers."

For his part, Herzfeld stated in the interview for this book that he was curious why Universal wouldn't take on Roach as the director because, "Once you get a director with a little heat on board, then it becomes more real." But he added, "They wanted me to take another pass [at the script] and my recollection is that before I got into the script again, or maybe it just kind of landed in neutral, I can't quite remember, but it didn't matter because somebody, probably at CAA, got it to Bob Cooper, who was running DreamWorks. He loved it and slipped it to Spielberg."

It still boggles the mind that an agency would take a script draft commissioned by one studio based on a script being worked on at that studio and send it to another as if it were free and clear to be made by the second studio. But Universal was dragging his feet and Herzfeld was not about to give up a chance on what he had already realized would be a very commercial property. Telling his tale of how *Meet the Parents* came about, Jim Herzfeld comes off as a man stridently defending his territory all the while avoiding as best he can the actual history of that territory he essentially lucked into. It's as if he believes in the purity of his carefully constructive narrative, a narrative created to deflect from that history.

Did he know the full journey of *Meet the Parents* and decided to retain only those bits of it that served his narrative? Or was he never privy to all that transpired on the way to that project getting into his hands? Never once in his interview for this book did he mention the script Greg and Mary Ruth wrote for Universal (that is essentially a template for his draft). Perhaps he never saw the first Universal draft, though Nancy says that, even if he didn't see the actual script when discussing it with him, she referred often to what was in that script. And so much of what was in the final movie could be traced back to Greg and Mary Ruth's script for the original film, if not in execution, most certainly in concept.

Herzfeld's memories are surprisingly clear on details outside of Universal, and he remembers it as a heady time. "Spielberg loved it and immediately said, 'Find this guy! Get this script! Make him an overall deal!' It was like crazy all of a sudden…you know, seven-figure guarantee, multiple years. All that."

On a script still under option at Universal no less.

As he remembers it, Herzfeld met up with Spielberg on the set of *The Insider*. They talked for almost an hour, Spielberg, *Meet the Parents* script in hand, enthusiastic about making the movie.

"As the meeting's about to end, he kind of looks down and goes, 'I'm gonna tell you something but you have to keep it a secret. I think I may direct this.'"

It's easy to imagine how exciting this was for Herzfeld. Here he had been signed up to work on a script under development at Universal, and now his draft was being wooed by a famous director at another studio. He kept mum about the possibility of Spielberg directing, not even telling his wife. "She's not even in the business, and can keep a secret, but when the most powerful man in Hollywood tells me to do something or not do something, I'm gonna do or not do it."

Once Spielberg had decided to direct it, he also decided that he wanted Jim Carrey for the role of Greg. No doubt it was shortly after this that word hit the trades and Greg Glienna and those developing the movie at Universal were left scratching their heads.

Jim Carrey in the role of Greg would have brought a completely different energy to the movie, but it remains unclear how successful that energy would have been. Carrey has proven himself to be a very good actor, but he does have a particular comedy style, and it's broader than what many involved with the *Meet the Parents* project at Universal felt would work. It certainly isn't the unassuming everyman energy that Nancy was looking for with the character of Greg.

According to Herzfeld, when Roach found out about Spielberg, he was disappointed but also understood. "Good for you man," Jim remembers the director telling him. "If I'm gonna get knocked out by somebody, Spielberg's probably the guy to do it."

Jim Herzfeld understood that his draft would need some changes now that Jim Carrey was involved. "I met with Spielberg and Carrey at Spielberg's house." They went over some notes but from what Jim remembers, the script didn't change all that much. "I wrote at least two passes at the script with Jim Carrey as Greg. Mostly just wrote some set pieces that were more physical. Jim Carrey-like. One of the gags I wrote was that he had somehow clogged the toilet and it was a really inopportune place and time." With the water rising, the character Greg panics and eventually takes his pants off to use himself as a human plug.

Again, the result of the gag is much broader, but Herzfeld may have forgotten that the core of the gag had already been used in the original 1992 *Meet the Parents* when Greg also finds himself clogging the toilet at the house of his girlfriend's parents.

As Herzfeld remembered it, the project seemed like a go, but as the weeks wore on, a few issues seemed to be blanching a little of Spielberg's original enthusiasm. According to Herzfeld the director had been working heavily during the mid-90s wearing both director and producer hats, as well as helping establish DreamWorks. His wife, Kate Capshaw, gave birth to their child Destry and was hoping her husband would ease up on his schedule and spend more time with his family.

There was another concern about the project weighing on Spielberg's mind that had more to do with ego, then a hectic schedule. "He said this to me early on," Herzfeld explained, "'You know, I made a comedy once and it didn't work out so well.'"

That comedy was the notorious *1941*. Released in 1979, the film did not do well at the box office in North America, but worldwide, it came in at $94 million, returning a profit on its budget of $35 million. Still, after creating a reputation for massive blockbusters with *Jaws*, and *Close Encounters of The Third Kind*, *1941*'s box office take just wasn't considered good enough for a Spielberg film. Plus, the critics savaged the film which no doubt made Spielberg a little gun-shy when it came to considering pure comedies in the future.

"I didn't think it was that bad," Herzfeld stated of the movie, "but he was kind of like, 'Do I go there again? Does the golden boy of Hollywood go back to his Achilles tendon and try to hit one out of the park this time?'"

The answer was, "No."

Since working with Spielberg was the key interest for Carrey to take on the project, the actor was no longer interested once the director had backed out. He left too, but not without bequeathing to the movie one of its most beloved running gags.

"When I met with them, they asked why I'd never given Greg a last name," Herzfeld recalled. "I told them, 'We could give him one. I just didn't have a moment where I really thought it needed to be mentioned. I'll think of one and whatever it is it's going to be embarrassing, right?' And then Jim Carrey goes, 'Yeah, like Focker.' And I go, 'Exactly.' So, it was me saying, 'Let's come up with something embarrassing.' And Jim Carrey saying the MadLib of 'Focker' and it stuck."

It is interesting to note that Greg Glienna and Mary Ruth Clark never gave their character of Greg a last name either in the original film. And the last name of Pam's family was Burns, which Herzfeld altered slightly to Byrnes for the 2000 film.

Spielberg and Carrey's brief involvement with *Meet the Parents* would explain why, in October 2000, when Ben Stiller (along with Jay Roach and Robert De Niro) was interviewed by Steven Daly of Entertainment Weekly, Stiller indicated that when he first got it, "The script needed a lot of work. There was all this broad stuff written for Jim Carrey. We did an initial read-through and even though we'd all kind of committed, it could have not happened."

Presumably, if the Carrey gags, weren't toned down a bit.

Still, there's that question in the narrative as to how a writer presumably under contract with Studio A, could start to make deals with Studio B for a draft of a script still in development at Studio A. When asked if that was a normal thing in the industry, Jim Herzfeld understood the confusion. "That's not normal," he explained. "What I think happened was that there were a couple of executives, like Kevin Misher and Mary Parent who were championing the project. So, while they were mulling over how to get it to the point where Ron Meyer, who was running the studio then, would greenlight the movie, it got into Spielberg's hands. I'm pretty sure what happened was that Ron Meyer was just minding his own business running Universal when the phone rang and it was Steven or somebody from DreamWorks who probably said, 'Hey Ron, you got a script called Meet the Parents.' And I'm sure Ron Meyer said, 'Yes,' but his thought bubble was, 'I do? Never heard of it!'"

Essentially, Herzfeld believed that not saying "yes" to Jay Roach earlier led DreamWorks into the door when it got to Spielberg. And while Spielberg decided against directing, Spielberg's company told Universal they wanted in on distribution. "You guys can keep domestic, we're taking everything else. Foreign and everything."

"I think I'm right about this," Herzfeld claimed, "but it was a very expensive delay on Universal's part because they had to share the revenue on what turned out to be between the three of those movies, a billion-dollar box office franchise."

Suffer the Long Night

Around the time it had become obvious that the *Meet the Parents* script was being shopped around, the second option at Universal was coming up for renewal. At that point, Universal still seemed to be sitting on their hands about getting the movie made; one possible reason that Jim Herzfeld felt so emboldened to turn to another studio. But if Greg Glienna and Mary Ruth Clark didn't re-up the option, then nothing was going to happen. They would be free agents again to shop their project to other studios. Since some heat had been generated with Spielberg and Carrey's reported interest in it, it was possible that other studios might be interested in taking a better look at it.

As Nancy remembers after looking at her notes from the time, while Jim was getting paid a large amount of money, he was not attending to the main problems with the script. "At that point, I find out that Jay Roach and Jim Herzfeld have been having meetings to discuss making the movie and then they phone me to tell me they're working together. The rights expire and Jim and Jay approach Greg and make all these promises telling him that Misher sucks, he'll never get it off the ground."

Greg consulted with Nancy and she asked him, "Do you want to see what Universal will do, or do you want to take advantage of the buzz it has now and shop it around to another studio?"

"He let it be my decision out of loyalty," Nancy stated. "All the while Kevin Misher was promising me he was going to make it. So, I opted to stay at Universal."

A difficult decision since after Spielberg's interest became known, other studios, including Disney, were expressing an interest in the project.

The decision was understandable though. Taking the script to a new studio would mean starting over again. Universal might be dragging their feet, but they were inching closer to making it. Momentum was there slow as it may be.

Mary Ruth tended to go with whatever Greg's decision was regarding the script, being even more out of the loop of studio politics than he was. In agreement, the pair renewed the option with Universal.

As for Greg, he sometimes questions his decision now. At the time, perhaps because the project seemed to be further along than it had been, perhaps because he didn't want to lose the bird he had in his hand for those in bushes that might not be interested even with the buzz surrounding the project.

If Greg had had more experience in Hollywood, he might have chosen a different path. Perhaps he would have been the one sending the script out to anyone who would look at it. With his focus by then on the career he had decided to pursue, screenwriting, he was content to let it ride and let the studio work its magic.

It was of course a gratifying decision for Nancy who had been doing her best to guide this project through the choppy waters of an uncertain studio. After the years she'd spent trying to convince people that this could be a "tentpole movie," it was nice to see people finally starting to take the idea seriously.

Considering her efforts, though, how little Nancy appears in the story that Jim Herzfeld weaves is interesting. His claims that he never met her could be a matter of semantics since indeed, the two never met face to face. With Nancy based out of the East Coast, the majority of her contact with Jim was over the phone as they went over the script. She remembered one conversation that she had with him while she was driving as they argued over softening up the character of Greg. He was resistant to the change.

It is perhaps understandable that Herzfeld was willing to fight for a property that both he and Nancy (and others in the saga) could see the worth of even if the execs at Universal couldn't clearly appreciate the potential. The troubling part was how willing he seemed to be to kick those others (others who had fought for years to make this happen) off the journey in his effort to turn the project into "A Jim Herzfeld Joint". He was a part of it only a year (per Nancy. Six months if you go by what he told Ain't it Cool News) before he sat down with Spielberg and Carrey in the hopes of getting the ball rolling faster than Universal was willing to roll it. And it wasn't as if after the meeting he went swinging back to Universal with the good news that he might have Spielberg and Carrey for the project. That in itself would have put a flame under Universal to get moving on the project.

There's a hubris here that while not surprising (hello! Hollywood) is none-the-less frustrating for Greg and Mary Ruth, the artistic parents of the film, who had to watch as their role in the history of this project was slowly buried by studio games and other people taking credit for gags and concepts they had created.

Greg and Mary Ruth would suffer a similarly frustrating situation with an intellectual property several years later.

In 2006, Greg approached Mary Ruth with another idea for collaboration. This time, for a play. The Merrillville Merry Art Players have a problem. They're attempting to present the suspense thriller *Suffer the Long Night* during a massive flu epidemic and 19 out of 23 community theater members of the cast call in during the day of the performance. With all but four of the roles being performed by understudies, it does indeed prove to be a long night.

Their play *Suffer the Long Night* was not your typical disaster comedy, as Mary Ruth explained it. "Most disaster comedies like that are about backstage humor. You know, like *Noises Off*. I remember Greg saying, 'But this isn't going to be backstage. We perform the play and everything that's gonna go wrong is gonna go wrong. We're not going to see backstage.'"

It would be as if the audience were watching actors from a legitimate theater group struggling to put on the play because not only did most of the main cast go down with the flu, but the stagehands are also working at a fraction of their numbers leading to prop failures, miscued sound effects, and other live-production disasters. The troupe tries its best but can't keep the suspense thriller from turning into a comedy of errors.

"Our play started," Greg stated, "with a lady walking out to address the audience: 'Good afternoon, welcome to the Merrillville Merry Art Theater's production of that well-loved classic *Suffer the Long Night*. One little announcement, due to the flu epidemic, we're missing 19 out of 23 cast and crew members so please bear with us.' And then the play starts, and everything goes wrong. We even had programs that were double sided so if you turned them one way they were like the fake program read 'Merrillville Community Arts… '*Suffer the Long Night* appeared in 1937…' The other side was the real program for our play."

To add to the interactive experience of the play, as the ushers lead audience members to their seats before the play, they offered hand sanitizer and boxes of tissue along with the playbills.

The play, directed by Greg, debuted in 2008 in Los Angeles and was well received playing in a few other cities. The biggest issue with the play was that it was expensive to put on and not very practical for a smaller theater to produce.

Six years later, in 2012, a play premiered in London, at the Old Red Lion Theater titled *The Play That Goes Wrong*, written by Henry Lewis, Jonathan Sayer, and Henry Shields and performed by Mischief Theatre Company. According to the plot, after receiving a large donation, The Cornley Polytechnic Drama Society decides to put on a 1920s murder mystery called *The Murder at Haversham Manor*. Despite their sincerest efforts, the actors and crew find themselves having to perform the play despite the many disasters that seem to strike out of nowhere. Prop failures miscued sound effects and other live-production disasters.

If that last sentence sounds familiar it's because it was used to describe the bits of business going on in the Glienna/Clarke play

Suffer the Long Night. The question is, was the idea Greg had so universal that others might have thought of it down the line without even knowing about *Suffer the Long Night*? Or did someone see that play, take the concept and "blow it up," as happened with *Meet the Parents*?

There are similarities in gags, but then both plays concern theater and so it's not unusual to think that similar gags concerning theater would strike various playwrights. There is one strikingly similar gag. According to a review of *Suffer the Long Night*'s debut, which appeared on the Onstage411.com website, "An entire scene gets repeated over and over when one of the 'understudies' keeps looping back to the start of the scene again and again."

According to the Wikipedia article on *The Play that Goes Wrong*, "In one scene, an actor repeats an earlier line of dialogue and causes the dialogue sequence triggered by that line to be repeated…several times."

"My God! It was so frustrating," Mary Ruth remembered. "Greg didn't even read it, but I read it. *The Play that Goes Wrong.* And I literally had to keep getting up, pacing, walking away, screaming, crying. It's the same fucking play! It's just blown up!"

Mary Ruth didn't believe plagiarism was involved. *The Play That Goes Wrong* originated in England, so it's not likely anyone connected with that play would have seen a performance of *Suffer the Long Night.* And *The Play That Goes Wrong* is as much a backstage comedy as *Noises Off,* where *Suffer the Long Night* had no backstage subplots.

Greg also seems pretty at peace with the idea that the similarities of the play were all coincidental. But considering their *Meet the Parents* experience, it had to have initially messed with their blood pressure to see their work copied without credit, even if this time unintentionally.

The Carrey/Spielberg involvement with *Meet the Parents* didn't last long, but later, Carrey would inflate his role in it all, telling

Larry King in a Dec. 15, 2008 interview on the broadcaster's CNN talk show, "*Meet the Parents* was something that I was developing... with Steven Spielberg. Yes. I actually created the Fockers in a -- in a creative meeting." An interesting claim when one considers that Universal had been developing the project years before Carrey got it, after Nancy Tenenbaum had shopped it around, after Clay Heery had shopped it around. Oh, and then there was the original movie itself. In fact, in 1992 at the time Greg and Mary Ruth created the original concept for what would eventually become the highly successful 2000 remake, Jim Carrey was making an uncredited appearance as Death in a film named *High Strung* still two years shy of his breakout role in *Ace Ventura: Pet Detective*. And *Meet the Fockers*, the sequel that introduced Greg's parents, wasn't released until 2004, well after Carrey was out of the *Parents* picture.

John F. Kennedy was once quoted as saying, "Victory has a thousand fathers" and there was no shortage of fathers to lay claim to *Meet the Parents* or elements within it.

Focker

The interesting thing about the choice to play Greg Focker, as the character would be named in the Universal remake of *Meet the Parents*, is how much his creative path parallels the creative path chosen by Greg Glienna, the man who portrayed Greg in the 1992 original. Of course, considering his heritage, Ben Stiller was destined for comedy. As the son of comedians Jerry Stiller and Anne Meara, he's been immersed in the business since he was a young boy, traveling the comedy circuit with his parents and watching live their appearances on popular talk shows of the day. His first acting job came at the age of 9 when he appeared on his mother's TV show, *Kate McShane*. Like Glienna, Stiller fell in love with movie making at an early age, making parody movies of the latest blockbusters using a Super 8 camera he'd gotten when he was 10. While in high school, he became a fan of the brilliant comedy show SCTV and through that, a fan of sketch comedy in general. It was a natural progression.

Like Glienna, Stiller didn't last long at film school, in his case UCLA, though he did take acting classes when he returned to New York City. In the meantime, he auditioned for whatever he could and continued working on his short films, which led to a very brief stint as a writer and performer on *SNL* and eventually to MTV offering him his own show. *The Ben Stiller Show* ran for 13 episodes on MTV, then went to FOX, where it ran for 12 more. The genius of *The Ben Stiller Show* lay in its expert satirizing of pop culture. Musicians, actors, movies, TV shows, all were free game to be sent up by the talented cast of Stiller, Janeane Garofalo, Andy Dick, and Bob Odenkirk, Greg Glienna's friend from the comedy circuit.

While the show was canceled, it did win an Emmy for "Outstanding Writing in a Variety or Music Program" and opened other opportunities for Stiller.

The same year that the original *Meet the Parents* was first shown to local audiences in Chicago, Stiller took on the task of finding funding for the film *Reality Bites*, which he co-wrote (with Helen Childress), directed, and starred in. The producer of the film was Danny Devito, who would portray Frank Manure in Greg Glienna's 2006 film *Relative Strangers*.

Reality Bites received mixed reviews when it was released in 1994 but did great business at the box office. Other roles would follow along with another chance to direct the 1996 movie *Cable Guy* starring Matthew Broderick and Jim Carrey, two actors who would later be considered for the character of Greg in the remake of *Meet the Parents*.

While his career was growing, it wasn't until the huge hit *There's Something About Mary* came out that Stiller became a powerhouse hitter in Hollywood. Co-starring Cameron Diaz, the way out rom/com from the Farrelly Brothers helped cement Stiller's reputation for being able to portray a nebbish everyman trying to deal with the extraordinary or downright bizarre behavior of other people.

The success of *Something About Mary* quickly put Stiller on Universal's radar when they began brainstorming names for who would best portray the hapless character of Greg in *Meet the Parents*.

Nancy originally brought up Stiller's name during the search for a director. "At the time, Universal said that Ben wasn't known enough. Then during the hunt, *Something About Mary* came out, and suddenly they were very hot on Ben Stiller. So, I got the script to him."

According to an Oct. 12, 2000, Entertainment Weekly interview with De Niro, Roach, and Stiller, Roach stated that once Jay Roach was attached as director, they turned to Stiller for the lead role. "We locked on Ben first. He plays a kind of earnestness mixed with anxiety I thought would be ideal for what I saw as a nightmare comedy. Ben has a worried look even when he's being charming."

While he was game to give the role a try, as alluded to in the previous chapter, Stiller felt the humor in the draft that had been written with Jim Carrey in mind needed to be toned down. Considering this, writer John Hamburg was brought on to help bring the script more in line with Stiller's style of humor.

Hamburg met Stiller in 1998 when the latter approached him at the Nantucket Film Festival to tell him how much he enjoyed *Safe Men*, a film Hamburg wrote and directed. A native of New York, Hamburg earned a degree in history in 1992 from Brown University before changing course and attending New York University's Tisch School of the Arts. His first foray into filmmaking was in 1996 with a short film called *The Tick*, which earned some cred at the Sundance Film Festival. Emboldened by the experience, Hamburg tried his hand at the indie feature film *Safe Men*, which earned only $45,724 on a $1 million budget, but garnered him some notoriety as a writer and director.

After their initial meeting, Stiller and Hamburg kept in touch, discovering a shared sense of humor, and eventually, Stiller asked Hamburg if he wanted to join him on a script that he was working on with comedian Drake Sather called *Zoolander*. The character of Derek Zoolander first came to life in a short film created for the 1996 VH1 Fashion Awards written by Stiller and Sather and directed by Russell Bates. A few years later, Stiller and Sather decided to try to expand upon the concept and write a full-length feature film for the witless supermodel and his fashion industry friends. "I read it [the script] and I went to a reading of it, and it was really funny," he told Mike "Box" Elder in a 2017 on the podcast Box Angeles. "There were some amazing scenes in it. But like most things it needed some work. And then I joined in."

Despite the efforts of the three writers, *Zoolander* at that time couldn't get off the ground, and the opportunity for Stiller to star in *Meet the Parents* came up, so *Zoolander* was shelved while Stiller went off to work on *Parents*. Shortly after he joined the cast, he campaigned to have Hamburg brought onto the production as a writer, to help tone down some of the broader aspects of the character of Greg and the plot.

As Hamburg put it, the response was, "'Ben, who is this fucking guy? He's made one movie that made $52,000. He wrote a couple of drafts of *Zoolander* with you, a movie that's never been made and sounds as stupid as anything.'

"But I had a meeting with Jay Roach and producer Jane Rosenthal and I pitched what I thought worked about their current script…Jim Herzfeld had written these drafts and it was hilarious and there were some awesome things and I just thought with those two actors, Stiller and DeNiro, there could be a slightly different tone."

According to Jim Herzfeld, "Jay didn't want Hamburg to come on and re-write me."

But Roach must have changed his mind since Hamburg was hired for a two-week run with an optional third week, and ended up staying with the production for eight months.

Initially, Hamburg was confused by the process since it was decided he would be designated as Stiller's guy. "I was like, I'd never worked that way before," he related in a 2007 interview for *The Dialogue: Learning from the Masters* on YouTube. "There's two people in this scene. Am I just supposed to write Ben's lines and then you'll bring the De Niro guy in?' And that's how I think a lot of Hollywood movies work. 'He's a specialist in this kind of thing.'"

Roach, however, wanted more. "He didn't know if it would work at all. But I think he had just watched *Safe Men* and read some of my writing and said, 'Just do what you're going to do.' And I spent a lot of time with him pitching him a new outline for the story. I mean a lot of the script was terrific and there were funny set pieces, but I had some new ideas, so he knew it wasn't crazy what I was going to do…The first act, basically, I rewrote the first act. I was like, every three days I'll give you another 30 pages."

Liking what he was seeing, the director told him to keep going. In fact, Hamburg seemed to become Roach's go-to writer. "I was in a great place," Roach explained during an interview an October 2000 interview with *Entertainment Weekly*, "...all the writers who were involved remained involved. They were all reading each other's pages, all calling in with ideas. But John was the guy who was kind of on payroll through the shoot. There were a lot of moments where new scenes would be coming in, and I'd be running back and form from trailer to trailer. Bob would give me something and I'd go, 'Oh, I don't know if that's gonna work with what Ben is working on.' So, I'd run out to Hamburg, 'Hamburg, we've gotta solve this.'"

Regarding Hamburg's inclusion in the process, Herzfeld later told Screenwriter's Utopia, "The good news, in this case, is that John has talent. He wrote some decent jokes and mainly ramped up the Ben-Bob relationship, putting Bob (De Niro) more in Ben's face and having Ben get on Bob's ass as well."

And in many respects, the delicate relationship between Greg Focker and Jack Byrnes is the engine of the movie as poor Greg tries his hardest to please a man who seems impossible to please. The question was, what actor could best portray that man?

The Man from TriBeCa

At one time the name Robert De Niro and comedy were not necessarily synonymous. Making a striking mark with his performances in such classic movies as *Taxi Driver, Raging Bull,* and *Good Fellas* (to name but a few in a career spanning 40 decades) the Manhattan native often portrayed somber, psychologically troubled characters in highly prestigious and very serious films.

With these performances embedded in the American psyche, it's easy to forget that one of his first roles was that of Italian immigrant Mario Trantino in the 1971 gangster comedy *The Gang that Couldn't Shoot Straight.* He would play in comedies throughout the next few decades, but they were frequently dark and psychological, like *The King of Comedy* and *Brazil.*

And yet, he also played in comedies such as the 1988 tour de force *Midnight Run* co-starring, Charles Grodin, the 1989 comedy *We're No Angels* with Sean Penn, and the 1993 comedy *Mad Dog and Glory* where, in this, Bill Murray of all people, portrays the mob boss while De Niro plays the mild-mannered police photographer.

Inside the chest of a dramatic actor beat the heart of a comedian trying to get out and were it not for his desire to lighten up a bit cinematically, Universal's remake of *Meet the Parents* might never have happened. It was his role as mob boss Paul Vitti in the 1999 comedy *Analyze This* that helped inspire his yearning for more comedic roles. Directed by Harold Ramis the comedy featured De Niro sending up his previous gangster roles as he portrayed a mobster on the verge of a nervous breakdown. The increasing frequency of his panic attacks leads Paul Vitti to consult a psychiatrist, played by Billy Crystal who is then put in the difficult situation of diagnosing a mobster based on his deepest and very illegal secrets.

The film was number one on its opening weekend, pulling in $18 million and going on to earn $177 million worldwide during its run.

It also seemed to usher in a new era for De Niro who began to mix more and more comedy into the movies he chose. Perfect timing for the production team behind *Meet the Parents* who were looking to cast the second most important role in the movie: Pam's father.

While Pam's father Irv Burns was portrayed wonderfully by Dick Galloway in the original movie, there was no sense of heightened tension between him and Greg (until the end, of course). He greeted Greg as cordially as the rest of the family did, and remained as patient as they did, for as long as he could, despite the escalating crisis that Greg unwittingly brought to the family. The family is unanimous in their willingness to accept Greg, and they are equally unanimous as fate drives a wedge between him and the family he had so hoped to impress. By the end of the movie, Greg's not only an outsider again, but he's also banished forever.

Curiously, the remake, which seemingly strove to make bits and gags borrowed from the original bigger in scope, decided to narrow the focus of that tension, concentrating it primarily on the relationship between Greg and Pam's father. Where Greg in the original is greeted by a warm family ready to embrace him, Greg in the remake meets a family, not quite as welcoming.

Or at least, more reserved in their demeanor (the movie would play on the "reserved WASP/meets urban Jew" stereotype throughout). It's evident from the first handshake that the chief source of tension will be the rivalry between Greg and Pam's father Jack Byrnes who spends the whole movie gazing upon Greg with an extremely jaundiced eye as if psychically willing the young man to screw up. From the moment Pam's father insults Greg's choice of a rental car (which is about three minutes into their first meeting), it's obvious that battle lines are being drawn and the "last man standing" contest has begun between the two. That, ultimately, is what drives the 2000 remake.

It was going to require an actor who could subtly project the energy of a territorial alpha male while also coming off sympathetic. After all, Pam's father has only his daughter's best interests in mind. Who better to project that then a man who'd been playing sympathetic mobsters for decades?

According to Jay Roach in a March 5, 2001 interview with Barnes & Noble, it was Universal's idea to engage De Niro for the part. "At that time, he was just finishing *Rocky and Bullwinkle,* which was quite a departure for him. I loved the idea. De Niro brings a certain type of humor even to his serious roles." During a Dec. 14, 2020 interview with Yahoo Movies for the 20th anniversary, Roach elaborated, "The thing I love about Jack [Pam's father as written for the remake] is that he's never right about anything. He thinks he's this killer spy who can read people better than a mechanical lie detector but he's really terrible – and Bob liked that."

It was De Niro who inspired the film's largest conceit, that of Jack Burn's being a former CIA agent. According to Roach in his December 2020 interview with Yahoo Movies, he and

Stiller went to dinner with De Niro one night and the actor discussed the research he was doing for another role on lie detectors and polygraph examiners. "...we were sweating by the end because you could imagine him putting you through the ropes," Roach related. "He even tried to get us to play the game of finding the differences between how our physical responses would be if we were telling the truth versus if we were making something up."

Jim Herzfeld stated that his draft originally focused on the mom as the one Greg would be irritating the most. "When you have a daughter that's getting married and there's a wedding that's being thrown, the mother's much more invested in it. Greg shows up as a wedding guest and he keeps fucking up the sister's wedding, so she was on him." Regarding the father though, "In one of my drafts, I went, 'Oh, he should be a former CIA guy. He should be a human lie detector.' That evolved from Herzfeld's vision of a father so obsessed with security that he installs cameras all over the house. "I think I just threw it out there and Jay was like, 'Wow! We should lean into that more.' And then De Niro read it and said, 'Yeah, that's what you need to do.' That's what drew De Niro to the script. If I hadn't written that, then De Niro would never have done it. And we got De Niro before we got anybody else."

For all the skill he would show at playing a security-obsessed father meeting his daughter's boyfriend for the first time, from what De Niro told Entertainment Weekly Oct. 13, 2000, "Well I wasn't sure about *Meet the Parents*. Jane Rosenthal said, 'We got this thing, and we're trying to develop it, blah blah blah.' So, I guess I kind of got pushed into it in a way."

It's hard to imagine De Niro getting pushed into any role he didn't want to do, and it does seem that more comedies have crept into his filmography over the past few decades, including the sequel to *Analyze This*, *Analyze That*, *The Big Wedding*, and, of all movies, *Dirty Grandpa*, and *The War with Grandpa*. He's also made guest appearances on television comedies *Saturday Night Live, Extras*, and *30 Rock*. To questions about his film career's change in direction posed to him during an appearance in November 2010 at the Doha Tribeca Film Festival in Qatar, De Niro viewed the business realistically. "Working with young actors is a necessary mix to even get the movie financed to any degree."

De Niro founded his film company Tribeca Productions with Jane Rosenthal and her then-husband Craig Hatkoff in 1989 at a time when filmmakers were rediscovering the cache of filming on New York streets (as opposed to Vancouver and Toronto, which had the feel of New York but at a fraction of the production cost). The company would go on to produce such titles as *Cape Fear, Wag the Dog, The Adventures of Rocky and Bullwinkle*, and *Marvin's Room* before *Meet the Parents* attracted their attention. An interesting sidenote about

Marvin's Room, which had started as a play written by a young man named Scott McPherson and premiered in 1990 at the Goodman Theatre: McPherson was Mary Ruth Clark's college boyfriend. "We had been actors. I went on to graduate school and got my master's in performance studies and he went to Chicago before I did. At some point, he figured out that he was gay, but we were still really close."

Marvin's Room spent six months at the Goodman before it opened Off-Broadway at Playwrights Horizons. Somewhere along the line, Robert DeNiro saw the play and decided he wanted his fledging film company, Tribeca, to produce a movie adaptation. McPherson was hired to write the screenplay for the film but succumbed to AIDs in 1992 shortly after it was completed, and screenwriter John Guare was brought in to prepare it for production. The film was released in 1996.

Just a few years before, Mary Ruth would be involved in writing the screenplay for another movie that would later be heavily influenced by De Niro. Unlike what would happen to Mary Ruth and Greg with the 2000 remake of *Meet the Parents*, however, McPhearson was credited with the screenplay for *Marvin's Room*.

"I tell this story a lot," Mary Ruth remarked fondly, "about two kids from upper Arlington, Ohio who would have brushes with Bob De Niro. One while De Niro's launching his production company. The other while he's re-launching his comedy career."

The consensus is that *Meet the Parents* more than likely would not have been made had De Niro not signed on for it. Certainly, De Niro's involvement encouraged Universal to take development a bit more seriously. While the involvement of Robert De Niro and his Tribeca Production Company was a boon to the making of *Meet the Parents*, it was bittersweet for Nancy Tenenbaum, who was watching the movie she had worked so hard to get made coming together, but who's involvement in the process began fading once De Niro, Rosenthal, and their company came on board.

"Kevin Misher apparently had been an intern with Tribeca Films," Nancy explained. "And at some point, Kevin said to me, 'I sent it to Jane Rosenthal and Robert De Niro.' I'm going to see if De Niro wants to be in it and they're going to produce it with you.' And I said, 'Okay, that's great!' After that, I think the only thing I was involved with was getting Ben Stiller the script. And then I didn't really have a lot of contact with them, to be honest."

"Kevin Misher made this statement to me: 'Don't worry. I'll get you back involved. Trust me. Even though you can ask any of my friends and they all think I'm a liar.'"

While her role in the project became smaller once Tribeca came aboard, Nancy is still listed first, along with Jay Roach, Jane Rosenthal, and Robert De Niro as a producer.

For her part, Nancy has been in the movie business long enough now to look upon the whole experience pragmatically. "You know, it wasn't a fun time, but I get it. I feel like my job was to get it developed to a place they [Universal] could see it. And also, to keep it in front of them to make sure they knew there was something commercial there. I was really big into making sure that it was a character-driven comedy. Not just set piece after set piece. I feel like I shepherded it [the movie] and was determined to have a real tone that was not too broad. And if not for me it would never have gotten to that point. And if not for Steven [Sodebergh] I wouldn't have gotten to that point. And if not for Jay or De Niro, it wouldn't have gotten to that point, right?"

And while her interaction with Jim Herzfeld may have grown contentious (or, per Jim, forgettable) during the months they beat out the script, Nancy feels he had a part in shepherding the film forward. Expanding the script and making it more commercial. Though, even then, higher-ups at Universal still seemed dense to its potential. "I don't think they got how commercial it was even after Jim finished his draft. Yeah, I don't think they got it."

With De Niro and Stiller, a go, it was just a matter of rounding out the cast. Teri Polo was cast as Pam Byrnes (affectionally known in the script as "Pamcake" by her father), the woman Greg wants to spend the rest of his life with, provided he can get Jack Byrnes' blessing. Blythe Danner, whose career goes back as far as De Niro's had the perfect grace to play Jack's better half, the ever-patient Dina Byrnes. Nicole DeHuff played Pam's sister Deborah, who's wedding the couple traveled home to attend (Sadly, in 2005, DeHuff would succumb from bacterial pneumonia that was incorrectly diagnosed at two hospitals as bronchitis and improperly treated).

Curiously it was decided to enlarge the family by one, casting Jon Abrahams as Pam's brother Denny, a character whose main purpose seems to be to advance the notion that Jack thinks Greg's a pothead because the jacket that Greg borrowed from Denny has the owner's bong still in the pocket. Since the plot hinged upon Deborah's wedding, Pam's sister had to be less flighty than Pam's sister Fay in the original 1992 movie. So, the onus of "the black sheep of the family" role was placed upon Denny to whom we're introduced after he crawls into his bedroom window stoned after being out partying all night. It's then that Greg, needing to borrow clothes after his luggage was lost at the airport, borrows the jacket with the bong in it that Jack discovers later.

Where Fay was more organic to the story in the original, Denny is there pretty much to set up a gag and is given little else to do in the film. For example, in the original, a similar gag has Fay put a reefer into Greg's jacket pocket while he's sleeping, which the next morning is discovered by Irv Burns leading Irv to question whether his daughter's boyfriend is a pot head. Unlike Denny in the remake, in the original, Fay, through other instances and her certainty that Greg can get her booked on *Star Search*, has more to do with Greg's growing discomfort over the weekend.

One role that was expanded upon and for the better was the character of Pam's ex-boyfriend. In the original film, her ex is portrayed as a nameless barroom bully, the sort so different from Greg that one wonders what Pam saw in him, to begin with (though the way other men in the bar greet her as she and Greg walk in to talk, it's easy to suspect that Pam was at one time very open to experimenting when it came to dating). He lasts a scene and then is gone.

In the remake, played by Owen Wilson, Kevin Rawley, as the perfect ex-boyfriend, adds to Greg's misery that weekend as insecurity makes Greg wonder why Pam ever gave the guy up. The fact that everyone in the Byrnes family still loves him (and he seems to be embedded in the family's life) doesn't help matters. Nor does the fact that Kevin seems to still be in love with Pam.

With all the pieces in place, filming, at last, got underway.

Credit Where Credit is Due

When principal photography wrapped on the production, drafts of the script were sent by Universal to the Writers Guild of America along with how the studio planned to assign credit on the screen. At this point, there had been six principal writers on that project: Greg and Mary Ruth who wrote the original movie and were hired to work on a script for the remake; Jim Herzfeld who was brought in to expand upon that draft; John Hamburg, who was brought in by Ben Stiller to tone the script down from the broad version sent to Jim Carrey and to work on the elements between Stiller and De Niro's characters; and two writers, Alexander Payne and James Taylor who would add bits of business and dialogue but would remain uncredited (and who seemed at peace with that).

A letter dated June 2, 2000, was issued to all writers involved in the *Meet the Parents* script process from the Credit Department at Universal regarding "Tentative Writing Credits" on the film. Sent out by certified mail to the agents of the writers, the letters probably took a matter of days to arrive, then perhaps a day or so more for the agents to tell their clients (or break the news in the case of Greg and Mary Ruth). The writing credit on the production would be as follows: "Story by Greg Glienna and Mary Ruth Clark," "Screenplay by Jim Herzfeld and John Hamburg."

"Signed Marcia Mahony, Vice President, Credit and Title Administrator, Universal Pictures."

Mary Ruth and Greg were left both stunned and confused at how they could be iced out of Screenplay credit on a screenplay they wrote. Although, there seems to have been some concern before Mahony's letter made it official. As early as the fall of 1999, Robert Wallenstein, newly engaged by Greg as his entertainment lawyer, was in contact with Universal seemingly to wrangle for credits. In a letter dated Oct. 22, Wallenstein explained to Keith Blau, a representative for Universal, that, "The attribution of authorship should indicate that the screenplay is 'based on a screenplay by Greg Glienna' and that the screenplay was written by Mr. Glienna with revisions by subsequent writers."

It's curious that Mary Ruth's name was left out of that request, but that seemed to be a thing throughout this film's journey. Even while the team had been hunting for a distributor for the original film years before, she was not made privy to the plans.

Be that as it may, on April 5, 2000, Wallenstein wrote Sally Burmester, the representative for the Writers Guild of America, West branch (the screenwriters union), enclosing copies of Greg's writing agreements and the option on the screenplay. "As you can see," Wallenstein wrote, "this project is based on his original screenplay as well as the version he wrote for Universal…Accordingly, we believe that the proper interpretation of the Guild rules will require that this be arbitrated as an original screenplay."

Judging from Marcia Mahony's June 2, 2000, letter the request fell on deaf ears.

"Story By" is a term that, according to the Writers Guild of America Screen Credits Manual, covers "…all writing…representing a contribution 'distinct from screenplay and consisting of basic narrative, idea theme or outline indicating character development and action.'" In many respects, Story is an outline or what is called a "treatment" that offers an idea of a plot, characters, and maybe some dialogue here and there to give later writers a direction on where to take the film.

Also, according to The Screen Credits Manual, "The first writer on an original screenplay is entitled to a shared 'story by' credit. That bylaw is called the 'Irreducible Story Minimum.'"

It was decided when creating the Minimum Basic Agreement, devised by the Writers Guild of America, which regulated things like writing credits, that it was only fair for writers who got the ball rolling on a project to get some sort of shout-out. Especially since it isn't unusual for the work writers bring to the studio to be altered by writers later brought onto the project by the studio. So "Story" credit puts a little salve on the wound by indicating that the first writer had something to do with the creation. Which is great if the work is dramatically altered from what was originally presented by the writer.

Even in his interview for this book, Jim Herzfeld conceded, "…there was no way Greg and Mary Ruth were not going to get 'Story by.' Like there's no way that anybody could not give them anything."

And that's especially true since the basic story is theirs.

For Greg and Mary. Ruth, however, the main problem can be found in Herzfeld's next line on that topic, "And that's beyond fair. You come up with something and someone changes almost everything except your basic concept…you absolutely have to get credit for that."

The comment is not as gracious as Herzfeld might have intended it to be. At best, it's disingenuous since he hardly changed "almost everything" about their script (or as he would claim, their movie, since his story is that that was what he was working from—the 1992 independent feature sent to him for review).

"Story by" without a "Screenplay by" credit made it seem as if Greg and Mary Ruth approached Universal with a "boy meets girl" outline and Jim Herzfeld and John Hamburg took care of everything else. It belied the work the two spent creating the original movie, and the work they did on the script for Universal, as well as fudged over how much of their ideas actually appeared in the remake.

It was a pale representation of what Greg and Mary Ruth had put into the production as writers. There would be no *Meet the Parents* starring Ben Stiller and Robert De Niro had Greg and Mary Ruth not furrowed the ground first with the original *Meet the Parents*. Had Greg and the team not pushed as hard to find a studio to back them on a new version. And had the writing duo not spent time writing the original script for Universal, a good portion of which Jim Herzfeld casually co-opted for the draft he worked on. This was their concept, their characters, and a good portion of their gags, even if expanded, which is what Jim Herzfeld was hired to do working off the original screenplay by Greg and Mary Ruth. (John Hamburg working off what Herzfeld brought to the mix). While Greg and Mary Ruth couldn't claim the final shooting script was a pristine version of their script, there was nonetheless a good portion of that script that they were responsible for. Especially since many of the ideas can be found originally in the 1992 version.

For a screenwriter, the desire for screen credit is more than mere vanity. It's about recognition in the industry that might lead to future work as well as how high the writer's financial stake will be in revenues for the movie since the residual percentage for a Screenplay credit is much larger than for that of a Story credit.

In this case, it meant millions more in residuals for two people who essentially lucked into the project after the heavy lifting was done.

Arbitration with the Writer's Guild of America would be necessary. But here's where the real problems began.

The Writers Guild of America

When it comes to relations between studios and screenwriters, the biggest bone of contention that has lingered since "talkies" came about is that of credit. Who gets it and what's it worth?

Once the 1927 release of *The Jazz Singer* showed what could be done with sound and movies, screenwriters became increasingly important to the movie industry, writing the dialogue that the actors were speaking on the screen. But while movie making truly is a collaborative process, the screenwriter always seems at the bottom of the list when it came time to hand out credit for a film, even though so much of the magic to be found on the screen originated in the script.

When "A film by…" appeared on screen, it was typically followed by the name of the director, or even the producer. The writers' names may or may not have been tucked away somewhere in the credit scroll at the beginning of the movie. Depending on how the producer felt.

Most people know who directed the classic *It's a Wonderful Life*. Do they know, however, the names of the other two people credited along with Frank Capra for the screenplay?

The name Alfred Hitchcock became synonymous with suspense yet how many of the movies he directed that kept people on the edge of their seats did he actually write as well?

A Cecile B. DeMille spectacular began with a script written by writers rarely spoken of when the movies are fêted.

Even modern blockbusters are known more for their stars, or director, sometimes their producer rather than the writers giving those stars, directors, and producers material with which to work. While that reality hasn't changed much over the century, the power of the studios has changed to a degree. Which is the key difference. In the early 20ᵗʰ century, when in many respects, the power of Hollywood was at its height, ruling the landscape were big studios started by men who recognized a good thing when they saw it and climbed on board what would very quickly become a money train: The film industry. At their heart, these were businessmen no matter how clever or creative they were with the opportunities that came their way. When it came to the art of storytelling, they had to defer to the creatives. In their defense, though studio bosses also had to make sure the money was there for the creatives to tell the stories.

As exciting and uplifting as they could be, when sentimentality was boiled away, as it often is in business, movies were a commodity that either made or lost the money that not only filled the boss' bank account but also paid for the movie factory to keep going.

That is and always has been the brutal reality of making movies.

For writers in the early 1920s and 30s, it could be a difficult time creatively. They were not under contract per movie, but rather per year with the big studio which meant they often worked on productions suggested to them by the studio. The term "dream factories" to describe studios was an apt one because the creation of a movie could often feel like an assembly line effort. If Warner Bros. decided it wanted to make another gangster film, a genre at which they were particularly successful, the execs turned to the stable of writers, most of whom worked from 9-6 every day from offices on the back lot, offering them a basic plot and expecting a fully scripted movie from that. (While they had a bit more prestige, often stars and directors were also little more than cogs in the studios' machinery to produce the product).

Writers A, B, and C would dash off a script and the studio would roll with it. Once filmed, writers A, B, and C might be credited. Or the credits could represent A, B, C, and a surprise D whom the first three writers never even worked with. D might be a family member, friend, or even the lover of a higher-up in the studio who never supplied word one to the script. Or perhaps the producer himself decided to share screenwriting credit with the other writers though his greatest contribution was to hand them the novel or play from which it was to be adapted.

To be fair, screenwriters were paid very well for their efforts. Especially in comparison to the trades people building the sets or running wires for lights and sound.

But at the same time, there was a serious dichotomy between writing for the screen and other forms of writing. When a playwright wrote a play, they were not only paid for the work but credited for it. A novelist received royalties from the publication of his/her creation and could retain ownership of the rights, as could the playwright.

A screenwriter, however, signed away the rights (or never had them, to begin with) to the movie they wrote and had to watch as the movie made millions that they would never get a taste of. They could sweat over a script for weeks or months and when the accolades came, they went straight to the actors or director.

When a ghostwriter writes a book, that person understands another name will receive the kudos. They're at peace with that, they went in knowing that.

A Hollywood scriptwriter in many ways was a ghostwriter against their will and watched others congratulated over a script that the writer was responsible for.

The formation of the Writers Guild of America (WGA) helped address these concerns.

The WGA began life as the Screen Writer's Guild (SWG) when the union was formed in April 1933. The seeds, however, go back even earlier when film writers grouped together to create the guild in 1920. Back then it was more of a networking organization where writers gathered to discuss issues they were encountering with this new industry of moving pictures. When the industry was starting with silent movies, writers pretty much delivered "scenarios," ideas for the director to film. When title cards showing bits of character dialogue came into play, writers became more important to the craft. That importance grew with the advent of talkies to the point where they were hired as wage-earning employees at the studios that were cropping up all over. As the popularity of film grew, and thus the power of the studios increased, it became more apparent that writers would need to figure out a better way to protect their work and their rights.

Of course, first, they'd have to establish those rights, and a union seemed just the sort of organization to help obtain them. With the Depression influencing the growth of unions, the SWG decided to unionize as well and did so in 1933, making a push to encourage guild membership. The more screenwriters that joined the guild, the stronger the guild became in its negotiations with the studios.

By 1941, the guild entered its first contract with the studios that guaranteed rights taken for granted now: Written contracts and minimum compensation. Control of screen credits through the guild. Arbitration. These were huge gains for writers who often labored namelessly for the projects so popular with the public.

With the guild growing quickly, in 1954 the SWG changed its name and broke into two branches, the Writers Guild of America West (WGAW) and the Writers Guild of America East (WGAE) after television and radio unions in New York were convinced to merge with them. Eventually, the studios and the guild were able to reach a consensus on one of the most important agreements: the Minimum Basic Agreement (MBA). The MBA, renegotiated every three years, involves the issues of pay, residuals, rights, and credits and offers the screenwriter basic protection in his or her dealings with the studios. It didn't raise the standing of screenwriters overnight, but it was a start, especially when it came to the idea of residuals.

Back in the 30s and 40s, few would have considered the possibility of "replays" of movies in theaters or on TV. Most probably never imagined video, DVDs, streaming, and whatever else the future holds.

The growth of the television industry was when the notion of residuals really came into play. As TVs entered more and more households, and broadcast hours increased TV stations scrambled to find captivating material to hold attention spans. Old movies became just the thing. For example, when a TV station showed the 1931 *Frankenstein*, Universal Studios, the owner of the movie rights, got a cut of the profits from the broadcast. The writers, Garret Fort and Francis Edward Faragoh who worked on the foundation of the movie--the script--not so much.

The WGA worked out a residual program that would assure member writers that they would be compensated for their work no matter how the studio decided to license it down the road. To protect the members, however, it would need to devise a firmer system to assign credits.

Demanding Arbitration

The guild's "firmer system" is subjective when one reviews the guild's policies posted on its websites regarding how rights are assigned. Even the act of joining the guild can be confusing. It has to be remembered that while both are branches of the same guild, each branch, East and West, seem to have its own requirements for membership, per their websites. For example, per the WGA West site: "We work on a unit system based on writing employment and/or sales within the Guild's jurisdiction and with a 'signatory' company (a company that has signed the Guild's collective bargaining agreement). Depending upon the number of units earned, a writer may be eligible for either Current (full) membership, or Associate (partial) membership."

It then goes on to list what kind of work can earn how many units to get the writer that much closer to guild membership. Another reason a Screenplay credit is important since it adds to the units required for membership in the WGA. Current membership requires a minimum of 24 units earned in a three-year period while Associate membership requires less than 24 units earned in a three-year period.

What the WGA East posts as requirements are a bit more nebulous; yet also don't seem quite as onerous. "While there is no single way to be eligible for Writers Guild membership, the general fundamental requirement for joining the Writers Guild is that you are hired to write by an employer who is a signatory to a Guild contract."

It's curious that being two branches of the same guild, they wouldn't have the same write-up explaining how membership works. But then, there are many curiosities in how the guild does its business.

Being hired by Universal to write the first draft of *Meet the Parents* was the ticket for Greg and Mary Ruth's membership in the guild so they were able to register their objections to the credit assignation and request an arbitration.

Arbitration comes up a lot in legal disputes. Frequently, people are encouraged, urged, or forced (depending on the situation) to sign a waiver stating that they would accept the out-of-court judgment of an arbiter if there should be a dispute. This happens often between employees and employers. Less formal than a court trial, a neutral arbiter hears both sides of the dispute, reviews evidence, then makes a decision. It helps unclog the court system and is less expensive than a court trial.

That is typical, legal arbitration.

The WGA arbitration to resolve writing credit disputes differs slightly. From a Screen Arbiters List, three people are chosen to serve on the Arbitration Committee. The people listed are members of the WGA for at least five years, or members who have received three screen credits. Each arbiter also gets a consultant to help them research WGA policy pertaining to the case while they're making their decision. These are members who agree to be included in a list and are essentially volunteering their time to help their fellow writers. The identities of each are kept confidential from the writers and the studio involved in arbitration as well as from each other, which makes a level of sense. This way, there can be no charges of favoritism (or other negative claims) by writers not happy with the resulting decision.

What this means, however, is unlike a typical arbitration, claimants are not able to present their case in person, clarify any misunderstandings the arbiters might have, or counter any inaccurate claims that might be presented in the "statements" of the other writers in question. All the arbiters have to go on are initial statements from each writer, and material such as the drafts of scripts, correspondence, and any other such literary (i.e. written) material that is submitted with the statements in the hopes of proving a point. Once an arbiter makes a decision, it's reported to their particular consultant and the Committee and then given to the representatives who had been assigned to help the writers craft their statements. They then inform the writers.

Writers disagreeing with the decision have 24 hours to appeal to the Policy Review Board (PRB), made up of three guild members from the Television or Screen Credits Committee. The PRB will review the statements of the writers but will not review the material submitted from which the arbiters made their decision. Their only interest is to ascertain whether the decision and the arbitration itself were conducted according to guild policies. (It makes one wonder how the review board can make such a decision without reading every piece of evidence relevant to the decision, but so it is).

The hurry-up aspect to this is understandable considering how there's a movie studio waiting on the result to prepare its opening and closing credit sequences for a movie soon to be released. Twenty-four hours, however, seems like the barest slit in the time window for a writer to review the arbiters' decisions (of which they obtain copies if they plan to appeal), comprehend the arbiters' decisions, then prepare and submit a rebuttal to convince the PRB that the policy wasn't followed.

Getting back to arbitration, from the date of filing, 21 days are allotted for the case to be resolved but writers have only 72 hours to gather the material to make their case and send it to the guild. Mary Ruth took the lead on crafting a response to the credit decision, dissecting the drafts of the script that the WGA used to assess credit, and presenting examples of why the decision was incorrect. It was a daunting task. If Greg felt a little out of the loop during the time the script was under development at Universal, Mary Ruth felt completely so, relying on contact with Greg to know how the project was progressing. Basically, she had to read through all the drafts, especially the final shooting scripts, and guesstimate how much of the material each writer, Glienna & Clarke, Herzfeld, Hamburg, Taylor, and Payne, were responsible for. Then she had to boil it all down into a statement of analysis and fax the whole thing to the guild.

"I'll tell you; this is the actual truth." Mary Ruth remembered, "I'm down to the deadline--had to get it in. How do you get it in? You fax it. I had a full office at that point, but my husband got the stomach flu. And he's heaving and being a drama queen though I will admit, he's heaving in the bathroom and I'm like, 'I can't help you! I'm finishing the arbitration statement!' Then he comes to the doorway and says, 'I'm going to the emergency room now.' I'm like, 'Fine Go!' I had to get this thing finished and faxed. And I did, I got it in. I pushed in on the last page and it all goes through then I'm like, 'What the fuck hospital did he go to?' And of course, we didn't have cell phones then. So of course, I'm like running around trying to call hospitals seconds after I send the arbitration statement. But my point being I wouldn't even let my dying husband—he was fine by the way; he came home that night. But I wouldn't even let my dying husband get in the way of my arbitration statement."

Surprisingly, before Greg and Mary Ruth could register their case, Jim Herzfeld had registered a case of his own, seeking to take John Hamburg off the Screenplay credit. To be fair, Herzfeld has stated he has nothing but respect for Hamburg's talent, but in his interview for this book, he was also very certain that, "Jay [Roach] didn't want Hamburg to come in and rewrite me." So, in later interviews after the movie's release, Herzfeld spoke of Hamburg as someone whose contribution to the movie was very small. Merely writing some dialogue for Stiller.

Nancy Tenenbaum understood that at the heart of the movie, the audience had to like Greg and Jim Herzfeld for all his creativity, couldn't seem to offer a sympathetic main character. The magic of that 2000 remake is the relationship between Stiller and De Niro's characters. The writer who ratcheted up that relationship, while still making both participants sympathetic, offered a lot more than a few lines of dialogue for Stiller, and that writer was John Hamburg.

Even more brazen, however, was that along with a desire to kick Hamburg off the Screenplay credit, Herzfeld also hoped to wheedle his way into "Story" credit. The latter seemed particularly cold considering how if granted, it would cut down the residual percentages of the one credit Greg and Mary Ruth had been allowed to have.

Mary Ruth offered a 20-page statement that included a "Breakdown of Individual Writer's Contributions" of the Final Shooting Script. This three-and-a-half-page breakdown pulled out elements of the final shooting script and attributed them to the scriptwriter that introduced it, comparing them to elements found in the script she and Greg wrote for Universal. In addition, as she stated in the conclusion of the main statement, "While the shooting script might differ 50% from our original screenplay, it is clear that no single subsequent writer has made all 50% of these changes." In consideration of this, they believed that "the appropriate writing credit for 'Meet the Parents' should read…: Written by A1 and A2." Or Written by Greg Glienna and Mary Ruth Clark."

According to the website Noblemania, "A 'Written by' credit is given to the person or team who both conceived of the story and wrote the screenplay. It usually merges story by and screenplay by."

One could easily argue that Greg and Mary Ruth fulfilled these requirements, no matter who came on later and expanded their work.

At the start of it, it seemed to be everyone's understanding that the arbitration would be conducted by the WGAWest.

By the time this chapter in his life had rolled around, Greg had moved to Los Angeles and was starting to make a name for himself in the world of script writing. Greg seems to think that he was always a member of the WGAWest, but when he became a member of the WGA, which he would have when hired by Universal to write the script, both he and Mary Ruth were still living in Chicago.

Which is officially in the WGAEast territory. Geography matters, apparently, when it comes to which branch you belong to as well as which branch should handle an arbitration. This is even though both are branches of the same organization and the fact that the four writers involved in the arbitration split the difference between the two branches (John Hamburg is from New York). Who knows, perhaps a coin was tossed to decide the location.

Ironically, both Jim Herzfeld and Greg feel their cases would have been decided in their favor if the West rather than the East had handled the arbitration.

Jim Herzfeld was certain that if the arbitration had occurred in the WGAWest, the case he established against Hamburg receiving co-screenplay credit would have been successful. "Most of the [Guild members] are West. And the West has a huge percentage of feature writers and the East doesn't. The East has a lot of late-night TV…so the people that they wrangled into doing the arbitration when you read some of the statements you could tell that they weren't really steeped in the process of writing features."

His point is valid. If an arbiter is more familiar with the contract of a TV show, which differs in many ways from that of a movie, it's possible they wouldn't understand the intricacies of credit that might give Herzfeld "Screenplay" over Hamburg who, one could argue, only tweaked certain aspects of *Meet the Parents* (which is precisely how Greg and Mary Ruth felt about Herzfeld input).

Greg believes that the West was prepared to pronounce his and Mary Ruth's script for Universal an "original screenplay," and thus, the required content expected from later writers like Herzfeld and Hamburg would be 50% (the first writers on a screenplay would only be expected to produce 33%).

It's important to point out at this time that, while writing this book, attempts have been made to contact the WGA in the hopes of gaining more clarification on the guild's policies and procedures, especially when it came to *Meet the Parents*, but the attempts have proven unsuccessful. The first representative contacted refused to even answer general questions, reminding that the case was completely confidential. An attempt with another representative to discuss general questions without naming the *Meet the Parents* seemed hopeful when the representative agreed to consider the questions. But once the questions were submitted, there was no reply. Even Greg, a member of the guild and a participant in the case, couldn't get a fruitful response from them.

So, unfortunately, much of what will be discussed regarding the WGA and this case will have to remain supposition based on paperwork regarding the case in Greg's file and what is found on the guild's Website. And unfortunately, the files don't give much of a clue as to why the decision was made to move the case from the West to the East. It was never really explained to the participants of the case.

However the decision was made, though, it was suddenly decided that the WGAEast would be hosting the arbitration. And they were of very different minds on what status Greg and Mary Ruth's script should be.

This is where the true confusion began as the WGAEast took Greg and Mary Ruth's original screenplay and decided that it was anything but.

The Goal Posts Have Shifted

Again, in the interest of impartiality (so that charges of favoritism can't be made) the names of those serving on the arbitration committee remain confidential, even from each other, as do the names of the writers involved in the case. The screenwriters are referred to in documents by letters. In the case of Greg and Mary Ruth's case, they were known as A1 and A2 respectively, while Jim Herzfeld was C, John Hamburg was D, and Taylor and Payne E and F. What I'm assuming is that B would have referred to Steven Soderbergh who did write a draft as well, but, like Taylor and Payne, wasn't expecting any sort of credit.

In the guild members' defense, determining credits seems to be a daunting task if a review of the "Guild Policy on Credits" on the guild's Website is any indication. There are many credit types to figure out, each with its criteria for determination. "Written by", "Story by", "Screen Story by", "Screenplay by", "Adaptation by", "Narration Written by", and "Based on Characters Created by".

For the sake of brevity, only the two at issue will be focused on at length: "Story" and "Screenplay" though the others seem just as intricate to attempt to navigate.

Part of the difficulty with assigning credit where credit is due could be due to the rules that "Story credit may not be shared by more than two writers." It is the same for Screenplay credit "except that in unusual cases, and solely as the result of arbitration, the names of three writers or the names of writers constituting writing teams may be used."

A writing team is indicated with the glorious ampersand so that in the case of Greg and Mary Ruth, their credit would read Greg Glienna & Mary Ruth Clark. And a writing team, with the glorious ampersand between their names, constitutes the equivalent of one name when it comes to credits. So conceivably, three or four names can be credited provided that ampersand makes an appearance at least once.

With at least six writers having had a go at the script for *Meet the Parents* (not counting the draft written by Steven Soderbergh), it cut down the chances for the slots allotted for Screenplay credit.

The two-writer rule might have been inspired by the old days when it seemed everyone and their mother could find their way into the writing credits. Once the guild and the studios agreed, continuing to allow this would severely lower the residual percentages for the actual writers of the script, which on one hand makes the rule understandable. On the other, the policy does open it all up to the very sort of issue that Greg and Mary Ruth were experiencing with *Meet the Parents,* and theirs is not the only tale of the creators and writers of a property being muscled out of Screenplay credit by writers who came after.

The WGA boils down the differences between the two credits as follows: "Story" credit concerns idea and basic narrative; outline indicating action; outline indicating character development; and theme. "Screenplay" credit concerns dramatic construction; original and different scenes; characterization or character relationships; and dialogue.

A reasonable, general foundation for an arbitration committee to start with. Once all the material to be considered is collected, however, it becomes a little murkier. Sixteen versions of the script, from the first draft written by Greg and Mary Ruth to the final shooting script, were submitted to the members of the committee who then had to pore over each to assess similarities and differences. Along with this were sent copies of the original movie, and correspondence between the parties involved. On the list of scripts sent out by Universal when the writers were originally notified of the proposed credits, at item #4 it states "First Draft Screenplay entitled Meet the Parents by JIM HERZFELD, dated 3/4/97 (123 pgs))." But this item comes after listed drafts (entitled *Meet the Parents*) by Greg and Mary Ruth, as well as the draft Soderbergh wrote, prompting the question: How can Herzfeld's be the first draft when three drafts existed before his? If Herzfeld had taken the basic concept of: Girl takes boy home to meet her parents, and taken it in a whole different direction, perhaps one could argue that his was the first draft of a screenplay based on that direction. But watching the 2000 movie, it's clear that he kept it all pretty much on the path to be found in Greg and Mary Ruth's scripts and their original movie. So, the "First Draft" designation doesn't seem accurate.

Still, there was a larger problem plaguing the case of Greg and Mary Ruth and what the WGA did next seems as questionable as awarding a first draft designation to a writer who came on to expand the draft already finished for Universal.

In a letter sent to another lawyer after the final arbitration decision had been handed down, Robert Wallenstein asked attorney Howard Fabrick of the law offices of Akin, Gump, Strauss, Hauer & Field if a case for a lawsuit could be substantiated against the WGA. In it, he stated, "The issue from our point of view is whether the guild erred in treating the screenplay my clients wrote for Universal as an adaptation or whether that screenplay along with prior material should have been considered an original screenplay. The guild flip-flopped on this issue numerous times before finally deciding that it would submit the material to arbitration as an adaptation of previously exploited source material. Obviously, this impacted my clients by lowering the threshold for sharing screenplay credit from 50% to 33%."

That previously exploited source material noted in the letter was the 1992 *Meet the Parents*.

There are two designations when it comes to screenplays: Original and Non-original. According to WGA credit rules for original screenplays, "Generally, an Original Screenplay is a screenplay that is not based on assigned material."

What is assigned material? Well, that can probably best be explained in the WGA's credit rules for a non-original screenplay: "Generally, a non-original screenplay is a screenplay based on assigned material written outside of the Guild's jurisdiction including, but not limited to, previously published material (e.g., a novel, comic book, graphic novel, play, or article) or literary material not covered by the MBA."

None of this might be a problem were it not for the percentages involved and how they differ between the two. For an original screenplay, to receive sole screenplay credit, Writer A1 & A2 (In this case Greg and Mary Ruth, the first writers on the project) had to contribute 33 percent to "any or all of the four screenplay elements and no other writer has contributed 50 percent to any or all of the four screenplay elements."

For a shared screenplay credit, Writer A1 & A2 would need to contribute 33 percent while later writers on the project would need to contribute 50 percent or more to any or all the elements to share screenplay credit.

So, in the case of *Meet the Parents*, Greg and Mary Ruth were in good standing, certainly contributing much more than 33 percent to the screenplay. But at an expectation of 50 percent, Jim Herzfeld and John Hamburg had a higher bar to jump over and if the breakdown that Mary Ruth wrote up was any indication, they didn't even make it up to the bar.

When the case was going to be decided by the WGAWest branch, it seemed that Greg and Mary Ruth's screenplay would be designated as an "Original Screenplay." But something caused the guild to change course on this decision and instead send the arbitration over to the WGAEast to handle.

Later communications from both Wallenstein and Mary Ruth indicate clearly that this was a complete surprise. Mary Ruth had just recently sent her statement to the WGAWest for arbitration when she heard the news that, "The goal posts have shifted" from

Lawrence Chance, a WGA representative assigned to help Greg and Mary Ruth through the arbitration process.

"And I was down at Columbus, Ohio in a minivan with toddlers in the back," she remembered. "I was in that middle section. And I was with my sister. We were on you know the speedy highway. And my cell phone rang, and it was Lawrence Chance. And he was informing me that they had shifted the goal posts on the arbitration, and this was a day or two after I had submitted the arbitration statement. I'm on this highway. With baby squalls going on and I'm like, 'What? I'm talking on a phone in a car on the highway and you're telling me what?'"

The goal posts shifted when the WGAEast decided that Greg and Mary Ruth's script was an "adaptation" of previously exploited material and thus warranted non-original screenplay status.

At first glance, it's hard to understand where this notion came from. Typically, it implies taking work from one genre and bringing it to another. So, for example, the 1967 movie *The Producers* was adapted for the 2001 stage show of the same name. *Les Misérables* was adapted from a stage show to a feature film in 2012 (after, of course, it had been adapted to a stage show from a book).

A Christmas Carol has been adapted to the stage, TV, and the screen any number of times since the novel was published in 1843.

The 2015 movie *The Man from U.N.C.L.E* was an adaptation of the 1960s TV show.

Audiovisual-wise, still one genre (TV) to another (feature film).

So, if anything, the 1992 independent feature *Meet the Parents* wasn't being adapted for the 2000 big-budget feature film *Meet the Parents*. It was being remade. Unfortunately, according to the credit rules, remakes fall under the non-original screenplay umbrella as well.

Yet the very people who wrote the actual first draft of the Universal film were the ones who wrote the 1992 movie. Technically one could argue it's a remake…but is it?

That was the quandary Greg and Mary Ruth found themselves in. Mary Ruth summed it up best in a draft of a letter she was considering sending to the WGA after the goal posts had been shifted. "We do not understand why the union has changed its position on the status of our short film and Original Screenplay created for Universal. We were rightly awarded Original Screenplay, and later informed that our contributions would be considered 'based upon source material.' But the source material, created by us, was a low budget short film! We realize our situation is unique but common-sense dictates that the creators of an original short film and original full-length screenplay should deserve the title Original Screenplay."

If the WGAWest was prepared to pronounce Greg and Mary Ruth's original screenplay, were they willing to break policy to do so where the WGAEast wasn't? Or, as Jim Herzfeld felt when it came to movies, were people in the West branch of the guild more in touch with the sort of unique situation that had been presented to them than people in the East who dealt more with TV?

Part of the reason the WGAEast was so ready to deem the screenplay an adaptation of source material could be because the guild was under the impression that the "source material" had been commercially viable, thus adding to its sin of being created outside the guild's jurisdiction. Of course, that was Greg and company's original hope, but, while it had some popularity, it hadn't even broken even, and it was only thanks to the Universal contract that Emo was able to recoup his investment. After its initial run, it played film festivals but didn't make a profit.

After that, the original movie, now on video, had been used to try to sell the idea to studios, as Clay Heery so valiantly tried to do. And once Nancy Tenenbaum got a hold of it, she used it to sell to investors and eventually, successfully Universal, on the idea of a remake.

While the physical script for the original *Meet the Parents* is gone, it was a script that Greg and Mary Ruth wrote as well. How much more original can you get? If anything, one could argue that what Universal bought from the pair when it purchased the rights to the movie, was the equivalent of a "spec script," a noncommissioned script that the writer hopes the studio will option. In this case, it was a movie that led to the option.

And that's something that the WGAWest might have appreciated better than the WGAEast.

What the WGAEast's decision meant, however, was that, during arbitration, no longer would Herzfeld and Hamburg need to show a contribution of 50 percent. According to the rules for non-original screenplays, they would only need to show that they contributed at least 33 percent to retain shared screenplay credit. Why there should be a difference in percentages required between original and non-original screenplays in this regard is one of those things that is hard to say. And hard to get answers on.

"That whole thing was just such a rug pulled out from underneath us." Mary Ruth said. "Gut punch. I think at that point I was really realizing, 'Damnit, we did not have a snake lawyer. We needed a snake lawyer.' We were two green kids from Chicago and now we were getting eaten alive."

The feast had just begun.

I Just Bought a House

In consideration of the change in status for their script, it's likely the guild gave Greg and Mary Ruth a little more time to get another statement prepared since correspondence between Bob Wallenstein and Mary Ruth, who found herself having to work on a new statement, as well as the final decision, happened more than a month from the date of the original credit assignation letter that started it all. And there's something important to point out: Mary Ruth spent weeks working on this problem. In an email dated June 14 to Robert Wallenstein, she attaches the first draft of their statement for the committee, but also indicates that she's having trouble "…getting a credits manual and a copy of our screenplay that is listed as 2 in Schedule 1 of Universal's Notice." She goes on to say, "I don't think our statement will be ready by early next week, as requested, if he [Lawrence Chance] doesn't send me the materials I need to make our case."

The tweaking of the statement continued, then her first attempt at a chart that illustrates points in the final shooting script and which writer/writers introduced them was faxed over to Bob on June 27. This is followed by a 19-page arbitration statement that same day. On the 28th, she sent over a five-page reworking of the chart. In the cover letter attached to this, she states, "I am still hoping to fly to Pittsburg in the morning to do a job, and if I can send all of this off tonight to WGAE, that would be great."

It would seem her plan didn't pan out, at least as far as getting the WGAE statement out because, according to a fax on July 11, she found out from Lawrence Chan that due to the change in their status (non-original from original screenplay), she would need to change the closing paragraphs of their statement.

Over a month her life was consumed by this attempt to save their credit rights to their movie, until July 31 when the decision of the arbitration committee was handed down. In the fax sent to inform Wallenstein of the 3-0 decision, she writes, "So I don't know if it's worth a fight, they clearly all seem to think all we provided was the source material for Jim Herzfeld's original screenplay." She ends by stating, "Greg isn't up yet, so I have yet to speak to him about whether or not we should pursue this any further."

The sense of defeat in that last line is palpable.

Mary Ruth's assessment of the decision raises a good point. There is enough room for screen credit to be shared between Greg & Mary Ruth, and Jim Herzfeld. And again, ruling on special circumstances could even see the third writer Hamburg in the credits. Residual-wise it wasn't ideal since the residuals would be split three ways (Greg & Mary Ruth would constitute one writer and thus would split that portion) as opposed to two but such a decision would be more reflective of who actually wrote the movie.

Yet never once is this considered in the deliberations of the arbiters.

Rather, they truly seem to think, as Mary Ruth suggested, that the script she and Greg wrote for Universal was simply source material for Herzfeld's "original" screenplay.

What would lead them to think this? Well Herzfeld himself may have played a part in that.

From the moment he got the job Herzfeld began building the narrative that his was truly an original screenplay, not based on source material outside of the basic idea of a girl bringing a boyfriend home to meet her parents. In his telling of how he came to be on the project, he goes from watching the video to negotiations with Spielberg to back at Universal with his original screenplay. A story that differs greatly from the story Nancy Tenenbaum told of his arrival on the project.

Even if he and Nancy hadn't worked over Greg and Mary Ruth's script for Universal, beat by beat, by his own admission, he watched the 1992 *Meet the Parents* (the very "source material" that caused the WGA to proclaim Greg and Mary Ruth's script for Universal a non-original screenplay), and a viewing of the 2000 movie shows just how much of an inspiration the 1992 movie was.

Two decades later, after the huge success, financial and otherwise, of the 2000 movie Herzfeld still speaks of the script like a man trying desperately to hold on to a stumbled-upon treasure. In interviews about the movie, it's about "my original script" and "the characters I created" as if he has to reaffirm territory that could be taken from him.

One could only imagine the concern he had during an arbitration, twenty years earlier, that may have resulted in Greg and Mary Ruth being given a bite of Screenplay credit, or him losing it and all the residuals to come.

According to Greg, so concerned was Herzfeld over losing the profit from a sole Screenplay credit that early in the process, he called Greg's then-agent, with a strange, desperate plea. As Greg recalls, "My first experience with Jim Herzfeld was when he called my agent, saying, 'Oh but Greg has gotta take story credit. I just bought a house!'" Greg had been in the office of his agent at the time and stared dumbfounded at him when the agent related what had been said during his conversation with Herzfeld.

Indeed, according to public records, Jim Herzfeld did buy property in Pasadena in 1998 upon which a house with 6,600 square feet of living space was built in 1999. One can imagine that the kind of payoff Jim Herzfeld would receive from a sole Screenplay credit on a movie like *Meet the Parents* would help pay for a five-bedroom, seven-bathroom house that would eventually be listed for $4.2 million when put on the market in 2013.

Of course, Greg was still smarting from the article that ran referring to the movie as "Jim Herzfeld's Meet the Parents" in the headline. "He took our names off it then," Greg remembers regarding the script, "and there was that article, 'Jim Carrey eyeing Jim Herzfeld's Meet the Parents.' So, I called the Writers Guild and they said, 'Oh yeah, he took your name off but we'll fix that.' But they don't do anything about it."

If he did call Greg's agent like that, it was a curious move by Herzfeld who, if he felt his contribution to the script was at a firm percentage, probably wouldn't have been sweating the decision of the arbitration committee enough to lead him to call another writer's agent. It was also a poor read of the room as well for him to think his recent real estate purchase would prompt Greg to take Story credit on a project he'd been nurturing from its infancy. This was about more than houses and residuals for Greg and Mary Ruth. It was about retaining the rights to a creation of their own.

Still, what might lead arbiters to think that Greg and Mary Ruth's script for Universal was anything but the first draft screenplay?

Herzfeld himself might have provided the clue in his interview for this book when he was told that Greg and Mary Ruth had written a script for Universal. "I guess that did happen," he replied, "as part of their…I mean my understanding was that the script that was submitted for arbitration was written after the movie [The original] was made. And I think I even made a reference to it in my quest to get the most credit that I could. It was like…what did they used to call it? 'Complete written transcripts. For a complete written transcript of our program…' So, it seems it was done after instead of done before hand. Which was a smart move on their part because you can't submit anything but a script to the Writers Guild for arbitration."

In other words, Jim Herzfeld claimed in his statement to the arbitrators that the material Greg and Mary Ruth presented as their script written for Universal and the remake was just a transcript of the 1992 movie. As if they sat down one weekend and typed up a script while watching the movie so that they'd have a draft to present to the guild as the script they wrote for Universal.

Which goes back to what Robert Wallenstein wrote in his letter to another law firm. "The issue from our point of view is whether the guild erred in treating the screenplay my clients wrote for Universal as an adaptation or whether that screenplay along with prior material should have been considered an original screenplay."

Presumably the "prior material" refers to the copy of the 1992 movie which was submitted along with the drafts Greg and Mary Ruth had written, and drafts from later writers. If the movie had been watched, it would have revealed where the inspiration for Greg and Mary Ruth's script for Universal had come from, as well as indicated that their Universal script was not a "transcript" of the original movie but rather a new screenplay (with elements from the original movie) for Universal to remake the movie. It would have also shown where Jim Herzfeld got many of his ideas for his later draft.

According to the Screen Credits Manual of the guild though, only literary material is considered during arbitration. Arbiters will read scripts, outlines, emails, etc., but watching a copy of a movie at the heart of the case would not be considered. And since Greg and Mary Ruth didn't have copies of the script they wrote for the original *Meet the Parents*, they had nothing but the movie to prove that the script they wrote for Universal was not exactly the same and was obviously written for a remake.

If the arbiters didn't watch the movie, is it possible that it was easier for them to believe Jim Herzfeld's assertions that the drafts being submitted by Greg and Mary Ruth were mere transcripts of their 1992 movie, and not new scripts written for Universal? In which case, it might seem very likely to them that the next script in the line to be considered as the original first draft would be Jim Herzfeld's draft, which is how it was listed in the list of script drafts presented by Universal with the June 2 credit assignation.

For all its importance, the WGA arbitration process has left many a writer frustrated and angry. The confidentiality of the arbiters makes a level of sense, but consequently, the process does not allow for writers to correct any misconceptions arbiters may have about the issue. Each writer or writer team involved submits a statement that could be rife with any number of factual errors pertaining to the script's development, but the other writers involved have no way of knowing of that or enlightening the arbiters. A perfect example of course comes from Jim Herzfeld's admission that he led the arbiters to believe that the script submitted by Greg and Mary Ruth was a script they transcribed from the original movie as opposed to one they spent months working on for Universal. And in fairness, he would have no idea what they'd stated to indicate that the work he submitted was a blown-up version of their own.

Essentially the arbitration process, unlike other arbitration, takes place without hearings of any sort where the writers and the arbiters can clarify positions and come to a more informative decision. Rather, the arbiters chosen are presented with a massive info dump of scripts and communications involved in the project from which they have to weed out percentages of who did what to arrive at a decision on how the credits should read.

The system is ripe for mistakes.

It's that potential that led Barry Levinson, a 40-year member of the WGA, to leave the guild in 2014 when an arbitration for screen credit on the screen version of the Philip Roth novel *The Humbling* left him questioning the validity of the process. When Roth granted Al Pacino the option to make a movie of the novel, Barry Levinson, who would end up directing it, spent two and a half years writing the adaptation, and was hoping to share screenplay credit with Buck Henry and Michal Zebede who were brought in to help with the project, but wound up not being noted for screenplay at all. For Levinson it wasn't just the denial of credit, but rather certain flaws with the whole process that no one seemed interested in addressing.

According to what he told the online media Website Deadline Hollywood that year,

"When the decision came back that I should not be afforded credit and I asked to see the write-ups, one [arbiter] said I should get credit and explained why, another just said no and didn't specify. And then there was this third person, who confused many of the scenes and attributed them to the wrong versions of the scripts. Some weren't even part of the final version of the script. It was a very muddled critique that made no sense. It was just way too messy and inaccurate, and I asked the board to have this person read it again because I couldn't see how this was a qualified judgment. Two hours later, they came back and said, 'No, we think it's fine.'

Levinson, nominated for an Oscar three times for writing, insisted that if he didn't feel justified getting credit, he wouldn't seek it. But on this project, he did. "They're saying, 'Even though the judgment is flawed and there are inaccuracies, that's OK.' I cannot be a part of a guild that could display such disregard for the work of a writer." The director would ultimately choose a status known as "fi-core" or "financial core" with the guild, paying his dues and being covered by benefits, but with limited rights outside of that. He would not be the only one feeling strongly enough to choose this lower status in the guild over a case of arbitration.

When George Clooney came upon a script that had been frozen in development for 17 years, he decided to give it his personal touch in an effort to have it greenlit. That film was the 2008 *Leatherheads*, a film he directed and produced as well as starred in. There was a problem with the script that he mulled over while in Italy until he felt he knew how to handle it, changing the tone to a more comedic one and rewriting most of the film. According to what co-producer Grant Heslov told *Variety* in a 2008 story on the case, "One thing that you clearly see, if you read the original, the subsequent drafts, and then his draft, is that he wrote the majority of the film."

And yet when credit time rolled around, Clooney was left out. Both Clooney and Heslov believed Duncan Brantley and Rick Reilly should get first position, but Clooney's work on the script was completely ignored by the guild's ruling on the credits. Of course, part of his uphill battle for writing recognition on this movie had to do with the fact that he was a producer and director. According to the guild rules, a producer or director must prove that his involvement produced 50 percent of the script (as opposed to the usual 33 percent) for him to gain a writing credit.

As Robert Marshall, an entertainment lawyer, told the *LA Times* in 1996, "Very little is revealed in the process. The names of the arbitrators are not revealed. The final opinions of the arbitrators are not revealed. The statements other writers supplied to the arbitrators are not revealed. Everything is directed toward preventing accountability, scrutiny, and review rather than the contrary."

Marshall was representing Judd Apatow in his suit against the WGA after Apatow claimed he did not receive writing credit for 1996's *The Cable Guy* even though, he claimed, he wrote most of the dialogue and scenes in the film.

In 2011, Story credit for *X-Men: First Class* was awarded to Sheldon Turner (who, as it turns out, never wrote on the script) and Bryan Singer, and screenplay credit was shared by Ashley Miller & Zack Stents, and Jane Goldman & Matthew Vaughn. Not included in this were Josh Schwartz and Jamie Moss, who were the first two writers on the script.

A dispute of credits for the film *Thor: Ragnarok* illustrates how limited these types of rules can be. Only two writers or writing teams are allowed Story credit. For *Ragnarok*, Story went to Craig Kyle & Christopher Yost, and Eric Pearson." This left no room for Stephany Folsom, who'd been listed in the "Notice of Tentative Credits" that Marvel sent the guild, but whose name was taken off when the guild made their final decision. It's understandable perhaps. Kyle & Yost were the first writer team, so were guaranteed Story. As for Pearson, since he received Screenplay credit, it's possible the arbitrators felt he should get Story credit. Folsom's response was to tweet, "There's something very wrong when a major corporation is doing more to protect your interests than your own guild."

Her sentiments are understandable, though per guild rules, the hands of the arbitrators seemed tied, especially since she came onto the project later than the others.

In 2015, the arbitration for *Jurassic World* mirrored that of the *Meet the Parents* arbitration only, in that case, the decision was in the favor of the original writers. Universal's first credit pitch offered Colin Trevorrow (who also directed) and Derek Connolly a Written by credit, which designated that theirs had been an original script and not based on any other source material. One could argue that any *Jurassic Park/World* film made after the publication of Michael Crichton's 1990 novel *Jurassic Park* had the novel as source material, but be that as it may, the arbiters, in this case, decided in Trevorrow and Connolly's favor. There was only one problem. A husband and wife writing team by the name of Rick Jaffa and Amanda Silver wrote an earlier draft of the script that they claimed was the source. After a protest was filed with the guild, arbiters decided unanimously that their script had indeed been the source material and the couple should share screenplay credit with Trevorrow and Connolly, as well as have sole Story credit. Written by credit was taken off the table. Trevorrow and Connolly's appeal to that decision was denied.

These are just a few cases illustrating the frustrating nature many writers have dealing with the rules of their own union. According to a Dec. 23, 2010 piece by Jim Cirile posted on the blog Coverage Ink, "It should be simple, and often it is. About one-third of produced films' writing credits are arbitrated." That number has probably not changed much. Indicating that as valuable as the process is, an overhaul might be needed, beginning with the policies.

Burns to Byrnes; Dogs to Cats

Could the three people judging the material for *Meet the Parents* arbitration really have been so off the mark when it came to credits?

Arbiters do not rely only on the number of lines of dialogue that can be attributed to each writer. Also important to the decision are elements like, "dramatic construction, original and different scenes, characterization or character relationships."

Along with illustrating specific examples where Greg's and her dialogue, concepts, and gags were brought through the writing process up to the final shooting script, Mary Ruth broke down the final shooting script and calculated what she felt was a fair percentage of work for each writer, even those originally uncredited. By her figures, she and Greg were responsible for at least 50 percent of what wound up in that movie.

What she offered was that out of the many gags and situations that could have been milked from the movie's basic premise (meeting the parents), a good portion of the material in the final script was material in the original script she and Greg wrote for Universal that was used or expanded upon by later writers.

"The names are the same!" Greg declared of Jim Herzfeld's effort. "It's just that the Burns family became the Byrnes family. Everything was the same. But he changed the dog into a cat. Changed the wacky sister into a brother. You know, the fishing pole in the eye became a volleyball in the eye. You know that's a lot easier to do than to have a blank piece of paper. He probably made 50 times more money than I did off this film just by doing that."

Let's consider some of the bits expanded upon. As alluded to earlier in this book, in the original, much to Greg's embarrassment, the toilet backs up after he uses it. Trying to extricate himself quietly from the situation, he confidentially asks Pam for a plunger so he can take care of the problem without the family being the wiser. Not thinking, Pam instinctively calls downstairs to her mother, inquiring where the plunger is. The mother's response is heard by the father who calls out his own inquiry as to why a plunger is needed. Thus, any chance of Greg dealing with this situation on the sly flies out the bathroom window as the family calls to each other throughout the house in search of a plunger. It's an effective scene that most people can probably relate to and adds to the tension that slowly builds up throughout the movie.

When writing a draft of the movie with Jim Carrey in mind, Jim Herzfeld went big (and gross) on the plugged toilet concept.

Greg is plagued by a malfunctioning toilet in the Universal movie, but this drawn-out gag involves Greg being warned not to flush the toilet when he first arrives (but never told why) in the room he's given to stay in. Also involved is the family pet, a cat that uses the toilet in said bathroom (and apparently can flush it), and a full septic tank that ends up turning the backyard where they plan to hold Pam's sister's wedding into a bog of human waste.

Again, the concept was expanded upon, but the idea of a toilet adding to Greg's misery can first be scene in the 1992 film.

Speaking of Pam's sister's wedding, in the original script, while Greg is admiring Mr. Burns' prize fishing pole as they discuss a fishing trip they intend to take, he accidentally casts the line and the hook hits Mrs. Burns in the eye. Mrs. Burns spends the rest of the movie wearing an eye patch, a constant reminder to Greg of how the weekend is faring.

In the remake, Mrs. Byrnes luckily avoids this fate, but during a pool volleyball game, after being goaded by friends of the Byrnes, Greg takes part in a well-timed spike that sends the volleyball hurtling down toward Pam's sister's face. The result is a ripe black eye, which is typically not a look a bride hopes to have on her fast-approaching wedding day.

It was Pam's sister, not her mother, and a volleyball to the eye, not a fish hook, but it's doubtful the remake's version of Greg causing an eye injury to one of the family as part of his weekend from hell was dreamed up without a little inspiration.

One scene in the 2000 remake turned out to be a mash-up of bits and concepts from the original movie.

In the original, as Mr. Burns tries to gauge Greg's responsibility when it comes to money, Greg responds to a question with a well-worn adage. "I believe a penny saved is a penny earned."

Silence falls upon the room and without a word, Mr. Burns rises from his chair and exits. Pam and her mom explain to a confused Greg that the name of Mr. Burns' deceased mother was Penny and he keeps her ashes in an urn. One of those innocent statements that no unsuspecting guest would imagine could be anything more.

And thus, we learn of Mr. Burns' slightly obsessive affection for his mother. Later he brings Greg to the room that he's turned into a shrine to his mother where the urn holding her ashes rests upon a pedestal in front of a large portrait of the woman. The urn eventually falls victim to the curse of disasters from which Greg is suffering.

This is one of the scenes Greg took the time to reshoot when he realized at the first screening that the audience was way ahead of him when it came to the fate of the urn. Reshot, the scene gets a huge laugh from a stunned audience who so anticipated the realization of their assumption that they never saw the actual cause coming.

Also, in the original, during a family dinner, Greg spills a glass of wine near the roast that Mrs. Burns has just placed on the table. Greg's attempts to sop up the liquid wind up with him causing the roast to fall on the floor where it's devoured instead by Bingo, the family dog.

In the 2000 remake, it was decided to reveal Mr. Byrnes' obsession with his dead mother over a dinner that also ends regretfully thanks to a family pet. While Mr. Byrnes doesn't have a private room set aside as a shrine for the mother (though he does have a private room set aside for mementos of his CIA days), he does have his mother's ashes in an urn in a shrine of sorts over the mantel piece. Next to it is a plate that he intends to have engraved on it a poem he's written to proclaim the affection he has for his mother. In the original, Greg is introduced to the solemnity of the dad's feelings when he takes him to view the urn. In the remake, Mr. Byrnes reads the poem that he plans to engrave on the urn. When Greg opens a bottle of bubbly he bought for the family, the champagne cork flies like a bullet straight for the urn which goes crashing to the ground. Instinct taking over, Jinx, the beloved family cat, goes to the ashes in a pile on the floor and does his business.

Dad's obsession with his mother. His mom's ashes kept in a sacred space. A dinner that goes wrong. Destruction of the ashes by Greg. A mischievous pet causing a problem that is later in jeapordy. These beats appear in both the original movie (and the script Greg and Mary Ruth wrote for Universal) and the final shooting script. The difference is basically window dressing. And Mr. B's obsession with his mother's ashes is such a unique idea, that in this case, it's hard to believe lightning struck twice during Jim Herzfeld's writing process.

There's even a gag that in an October 2000 interview with Entertainment Weekly, Jay Roach claims was thought up by Stiller. "One of the great scenes that Ben helped with," the director stated, "was the car chase. We couldn't afford a prolonged, full-on chase, so Ben had the idea of doing a *suburban* chase, where you weren't allowed to go very fast or very far between stoplights."

And that is an amusing scene. The thing is a very similar gag occurs in the 1992 film.

In the original movie, Pam's ex-boyfriend approaches Pam and Greg in a bar and challenges Greg to a fight. Unwilling to take part, Greg pulls Pam from the bar and to the car. The brute of an ex follows them with his friends and shakes the small car around trying to get in. When Greg finally gets the key in the ignition and drives away, the boyfriend and company give chase, but Greg, unwilling to break traffic laws despite the danger, drives the speed limit and stops at every red light. Once he stops, the pursuers leave their car and begin shaking the couple's car again until the light turns green and Greg pulls away, the boyfriend and his friends running back to their car to give hot pursuit (or as hot a pursuit as it can be at 25 MPH). This happens for a few more lights until at last Greg and Pam elude the gang. The scene is so ridiculous, especially when Greg stops and the gang gets out to harass them, that by the last light, the audience is screaming.

In the 2000 remake, realizing his plan to fool the family with a fake Jinx until he can find the real one has gone awry, Greg leaves the rehearsal dinner in the hopes of getting back to the house first. Having discovered his plan, Mr. Byrnes rushes the family out to get in the car so that they can get there before Greg. They speed along, but since this is a busier section of town, red lights occur every block or two, causing the two cars to squeal to a halt and allowing Stiller and De Niro to stare at each other menacingly until the light turns green and they can speed off only to stop at the next light. This is also a funny scene, but again, the meat of the comedy, trying to conduct a chase while adhering to the rules of the road, had been done in the original.

It wouldn't be unusual for two comedy minds to think up similar gags. Greg Glienna's sister found Stiller's performance of the hapless boyfriend in the 2000 remake surprisingly similar to Greg's deadpan performance in the 1992 original, making it seem as if Stiller may have comedic sensibilities similar to Greg's.

It just seems curious that those similar gags appeared in versions of the same movie supposedly without Stiller having any awareness of the original. If Stiller had seen a copy of the original movie, might that bit have lodged in his head only to shake loose when needed?

Mary Ruth was thorough in her assessment of what writer was responsible for what. She was so thorough that when Greg's lawyer at the time saw it, he told her, "If you ever want to switch careers, I could use someone with your attention to detail." And her assessment indicates clearly that their script; their ideas are somewhere in practically every frame of the 2000 Universal remake, whether used outright or altered. How could that not be apparent to the arbiters?

Unless, again, the arbiters were led to believe that the scripts Greg and Mary Ruth wrote for Universal were actually just transcripts of the 1992 movie, made outside of the WGA jurisdiction. This might be why they didn't look very closely at the script the pair wrote for Universal. Especially if they thought that the 1992 was previously exploited source material as the WGAEast claimed (and thus confirming the belief that non-original aspect of Greg and Mary Ruth's scripts). It's interesting to note that around this time an email was sent to the WGA referencing National Lampoon's deal to distribute the original, implying that the original movie was exploited (i.e. commercial) source material. It's not known where the email originated from, but Mary Ruth in one of the drafts she prepared for the arbitration, felt the need to address the National Lampoon deal and how it ultimately fell through. "While we were delighted that National Lampoon felt that the short film was worthy of distribution, they in no way followed through with exploitation or distribution of the film."

Reading the arbiters' statements, however, one can't help but wonder how seriously they even took the claim of Greg and Mary Ruth, at the time two relatively new members of the guild.

Arbiter number one acknowledged the similarity of story. "However, Writer A1 & Writer A2's screenplay is far removed from the shooting script. Essential story elements remain but structural changes in terms of 'opening up the story' are vastly different in the final draft (shooting script)."

But really, are they? It's hard to tell because the drafts of the scripts are gone. Neither Greg nor Mary Ruth (who did read through each one to make her chart for the arbitration statement) have them. The file I received from Bob Wallenstein contained arbiter statements and the back and forth between Mary Ruth and Lawrence Chance who was supposed to be helping her prepare the statement, but not the versions of the script that arbiters had to go by to make their decision. Versions may be on file at the WGA East but it's doubtful they'd be willing to present copies for this project.

To judge, we have only the 1992 screenplay as seen in the movie and the 2000 shooting script as seen in that movie, as well as Nancy Tenenbaum's assertions that much of what was found in the 1992 movie was brought into the remake script Greg and Mary Ruth wrote.

We do know that Greg and Mary Ruth were hired by Universal to turn their 1990 script written for the independent feature into a script for a movie with a much larger budget. We do know that they worked with Steven Soderbergh, then attached as director, and Nancy Tenenbaum, the producer, to Hollywood-up the script. A Soderbergh version is listed after theirs on the list of versions presented to the WGA. And from the Nancy Tenenbaum interview, we know that Jim Herzfeld was brought in to expand the script into a more commercial film.

And we have Mary Ruth's painstaking assessment of just what elements dreamt up by her and Greg were enlarged by the other writers. The basic premise: girl brings boyfriend home to meet parents, is there, and there exists a myriad of ideas that could have been used for gags and set-ups for such a premise, but much of what was left in the final script was unmistakably inspired by gags created by Greg and Mary Ruth.

It's hard to appreciate the originality of Herzfeld's contribution when his idea of it was to retain Pam and Greg but to simply respell Pam's last name from Burns to Byrnes. The dog becomes a cat which, like the dog in the original, ruins a family meal thanks to an accident on the part of Greg. The urn of Pam's grandmother is in a place of honor thanks to Mr. Burns/Byrnes' obsession with his dead mother. And the urns in both movies suffer a tragic end. Pam's wacky sister becomes a brother in the remake, both siblings in both films causing Greg a problem because of marijuana in a jacket. Fecal matter comes into play in both versions, it's just more disgusting in a larger manner in the remake.

It isn't possible to say that Herzfeld and Hamburg, the two who were awarded sole credit for the screenplay, didn't contribute a considerable amount to the movie. But out of the many ideas they could have used with the premise, they chose instead to use gags and concepts thought up by Greg and Mary Ruth and presented in their 1992 movie and the script they wrote for Universal. They retooled ideas already in the script.

Greg and Mary Ruth laid the groundwork and Herzfeld and Hamburg took all the credit for embellishments.

Essentially, an architect doesn't lose the right to say he designed the house just because interior decorators chose inviting colors and cool furniture to make it even more enticing. Those elements were chosen because of the design the architect came up with, not the other way around. And Herzfeld may never have even had a relationship with Universal let alone *Meet the Parents* had he not been called in to add to the script already written by Greg and Mary Ruth.

As the Arbiters Saw It

What Story credit did to Mary Ruth and Greg, using the architecture analogy, is turn them into two people who simply stated, "Let's build a two story-here," completely obliterating all the time and effort they spent in drawing up the plans and choosing materials for that two-story.

Arbiter 1's assessment only reinforces this.

Arbiter 2 acknowledges that Greg and Mary Ruth laid the foundation for the "…element of plot, story, structure and characters that are found in the shooting script." (You know, the movie) and feels they should keep "Story" credit for that reason. He/she goes on to say, however that… "the writers' claim that a sole screenplay credit should be awarded to them is utterly misguided."

And this might be where Greg and Mary Ruth overplayed an already (and unfairly) weak hand when they asked that the credits read "Written by Greg Glienna and Mary Ruth Clark."

The level of semantics that goes into all this is mindboggling. "Written by," "Screenplay by," "Story by," "Adapted by." Etc. It can all be so confusing.

In the minds of our two creators, "Written by" may have seemed logical since they came up with the story and the original script.

But one can just imagine how cocky this must have come off to a member of the WGA reviewing the material and thinking only in terms of "Story" and "Screenplay."

Since "Screenplay" seems to be the golden ticket, it's hard to understand why an additional "Written by" category has to be there if the guild isn't going to worry about who wrote the movie and go only by the final shooting script.

So that's a tough call. Greg and Mary Ruth wrote that movie. Embellishments that came after notwithstanding, the remake is there because they wrote the movie. But one can't argue what Herzfeld and Hamburg contributed to the final school script that would warrant the screenplay credit.

Where Arbiter 2 errs is in his/her assessment that "Writer C, I believe, deserves sole screenplay credit." For reasons I bring up regarding arbiter 1's assessment, there is far too much in the final shooting script that is there thanks to what Greg and Mary Ruth came up with originally to reasonably conclude that Herzfeld should be credited for it all with a "sole screenplay" credit. There was a screenplay already there for Herzfeld to work with, with elements he had no problem building upon. That must count for something.

Still, it seems that Greg and Mary Ruth's desire for a "Written by" credit caused a little bit of acid to come out. While Arbiter 2 acknowledged that "Writer A1 & Writer A2's adaptation and expansion of the short film 'Meet the Parents' lays the foundation for the elements of plot, story, structure and characters that are found in the shooting script…the writer's claim that a sole screenplay credit should be awarded to them is utterly misguided. Their execution of those elements, across the board, is entirely missing from the shooting script and their attempt in their joint statement to frame the screenplays of the writers who proceeded them as merely extrapolations and expansions on their screenplay was, in my opinion, unfounded and implausible."

So affronted by Greg and Mary Ruth's request for sole screenplay on their movie was Arbiter 2 that he/she couldn't even consider that perhaps, while they shouldn't receive sole screenplay credit, they could share screenplay credit with Herzfeld considering how they laid the foundation for the elements of plot, story, structure, and characters that are found in the shooting script.

Arbiter 2, however, stated a few interesting things that had to have been based on material submitted for arbitration.

To his/her credit, Arbiter 2 disagreed with Herzfeld's apparent attempt to weasel his way into "Story" credit.

If this comes off as a credit grab it's probably because it is. That Herzfeld thought Greg and Mary Ruth, who thought up the whole premise of the movie, who have the 1992 movie not to mention the script they wrote for Universal to back them up, should have to share the only credit Universal was giving them with a guy brought on to expand upon their idea was…well even Arbiter 2 couldn't get on board that train. "I would decline his request for a share in the 'story by' credit, as the 'basic narrative idea, theme or outline indicating character development and action' defined as 'story' in the Screen Credits Manual can be found in the source material and in Writer Team A's subsequent screenplay."

Interestingly, Arbiter 2 also felt that Hamburg's contributions did not warrant a shared screenplay credit. "…it should be pointed out that the overwhelming majority of his contributions were made between 9/10/99 and 10/3/99, roughly a three-week period. The ensuing revisions, while I'm sure they were time-consuming and hopefully wallet-thickening, are mostly comprised of dialogue polishes and location reassignments, and are pre-determined to a large extent by the requirements of the studio filmmaking process…I do not believe that Writer D meets the 33% new and original contribution required for him to receive credit…"

Ouch! Arbiter 2's belief that Herzfeld should get sole screenplay credit actually went against the Guild's original approval of Screenplay credit to Herzfeld and Hamburg.

John Hamburg was brought on the project by Ben Stiller who no doubt felt confident that Hamburg knew him well enough to help tailor the part of Greg to him.

Also, as stated in a prior chapter, Stiller originally received a Carry-ized version of the script that made him hesitant about taking the role of Greg. Knowing his friend's comic stylings, Hamburg would know how to…well Stiller-ize the role of Greg to the benefit of Stiller and the movie.

To her credit, Mary Ruth broke down what she felt was a fair assessment of what Hamburg brought to the project and while she and Greg should have received a Screenplay credit, along with Herzfeld, it wasn't a stretch to think that Hamburg should also receive it considering his contribution to the film. A lot can be done in a three-week period, despite what Arbiter 2 seemed to think.

Arbiter 2 does make an interesting comment. "However, the Guild, in this instance, also allowed as materials notes and faxes by Writer C [Herzfeld] pertaining to subsequent screenplays to the director and producer of the movie after Writer C was fired and Writer D & E1 & E2 were brought on…"

Writers D, E1, and E2 allude to John Hamburg, John Taylor, and Alexander Payne, the last two writers who remained uncredited on the project (and who didn't bother to put up a fight about it).

Now, back to Arbiter 2's desire to make Herzfeld "sole screenplay" credit, it's interesting that he/she does acknowledge that other writers were brought on presumably to finish the work that Writer C, Herzfeld, was fired from.

Essentially, Arbiter 2 seems to decide that the work Herzfeld did on the script should preclude Greg and Mary Ruth from Screenplay credit. But the work that Hamburg did on the script (much of it fixing the problem of Greg being unlikable) should not be allowed to overshadow Herzfeld's involvement, which Arbiter 2 has no problem stating should overshadow the work of Greg and Mary Ruth.

The comment, however, also begs the question: When was Herzfeld fired, and why? If he was fired. The comment implies that Hamburg, Taylor, and Payne were brought on after this supposed firing, so was Herzfeld let go early in the project?

At this point in the project, Nancy Tenenbaum herself had been shunted aside from it all, so she was surprised to hear of this, and could provide no information on it.

Arbiter 3 felt the credits offered should stand though did add the caveat, "The truth as I see it, is that the final shooting script could not exist in its form without the original short film's layout of situation, character, event and, notwithstanding the other writer's statements, tone. I am compelled by A1 & A2's assessment that the final script is their work, made much bigger and wider."

That being stated…

Arbiter 3 felt that, per the Screen Credits Manual that requires 33% of the writing is original, "I feel that any fair reading of the material would make the decision that D's contributions were not merely cosmetic. That he punched up the dialogue & made the father's role larger."

And no one can deny that the father's role becoming larger helped the final film. Though one could argue, how much of that is thanks to Hamburg and how much is De Niro. Arbiter 3 felt that "… the last 1/3 of the final script was his." (This might make sense too if, as Arbiter 2 claimed, Herzfeld was fired mid-project).

Despite his/her assessment of A1 and A2's work that, "…the final script is their work made much bigger and wider," Arbiter 3's end decision was that the credits should stand as they were.

Arbiter 3's paragraph-long defense of writer D's involvement in the project (and the lack of assessment for Herzfeld's credit) makes one wonder if 3 was less concerned with whether Greg and Mary Ruth should receive "screenplay" credit as much as he/she was concerned with defending Hamburg's right to credit.

It's hard to envy the position of those who agree to be arbiters in these sorts of cases. No doubt as in any organization, there are those who got a little thrill over the power their decision holds. But, for the most part, those members of the guild who agree to such extra tasks do so to make their organization better and to uphold the principles of that organization.

Unless there is proof otherwise, it does seem like the three arbiters, in this case, assessed the situation as fairly as they felt they could.

The question is, why not give Greg and Mary Ruth Screenplay credit too?

The credits would have read "Screenplay by Greg Glienna & Mary Ruth Clark and Jim Herzfeld and John Hamburg." Yes, it would have cut down Herzfeld and Hamburg's percentage points but would have increased the points for the writers of the original screenplay who were seeing their work hijacked.

Theoretically, members of an organization (the WGA) would be able to appreciate the importance of being noted on a screenplay they worked on.

Greg and Mary Ruth may have shot themselves in the foot by requesting Written by credit rather than simply requesting the first position on the Screenplay credit. Be that as it may, why were the fellow screenwriters involved in adjudicating the arbitration so myopic that they couldn't have suggested this in their final decisions on the case? Had Lawrence Chance, Greg and Mary Ruth's advocate for the arbitration, suggested that they might have a better shot at sharing Screenplay?

Ultimately what it boils down to is this: Greg and Mary Ruth wrote a wonderful script in 1990 and a wonderful, if a low-budget movie was made from that script. To get the concept out there to a larger audience, Greg and Mary Ruth offered their script to Universal. Universal asked them to write a larger script. They did, and Herzfeld was brought on to enlarge the script but seeing the worth of it all slowly created the narrative that it was his script, his concept. These were characters he created, or so he would infer. He had no concern with Greg and Mary Ruth and what they put into the end result. Rather, he tried to lighten their footprint in it all. He acknowledged that it was based on an independent movie by Greg Glienna but that was it. He didn't mention how Greg and Mary Ruth were commissioned to write a screenplay and how much of that screenplay existed for him to work with when he was hired to expand it.

It's hard not to wonder if Greg and Mary Ruth's status as Guild members had a hand in this. They were new to the guild with only one screenplay—*Meet the Parents*—to their credit. They were up against writers who had years' worth of credits with the WGA.

This is not to impugn the character of the arbiters in the case, but it's easy as an outsider, to wonder if the concerns of Greg and Mary Ruth, as newcomers, were not taken as seriously as those of a Jim Herzfeld or John Hamburg.

Again—conjecture—but it's hard not to raise the question of how fair was the arbitration that Greg and Mary Ruth received. Were the WGA and the arbiters at the mercy of rigid policies when they made their decision or were they just unable to review the situation as the truly unique situation it was? They stated that Greg and Mary Ruth's script was based on previously exploited source material not under the jurisdiction of the WGA. But that source material also belonged to Greg and Mary Ruth. Shouldn't this important detail have played a larger part in the final decision? As Mary Ruth described it, this was a unique situation and should have been treated as such.

Universal, for example, the studio that hired Greg and Mary Ruth to write the original screenplay were the ones who kicked them off the credit for the Screenplay and offered them only Story credit when the studio sent their tentative writing credits to the guild for acceptance (an acceptance the guild gave). Why? Again, if Herzfeld had taken the story in a new direction, one could understand. But he didn't. Why would Universal feel the need to ice out of Screenplay credit the two writers they originally hired to write the screenplay?

Curiously it was Marcia Mahony, VP of Credit and Title Administration at Universal who sent the June 2 list to the guild indicating Jim Herzfeld's 3/4/1997 draft as "First Draft Screenplay" (And didn't include Soderbergh's version in that list). On that same list, there were indicated two drafts before Herzfeld's that were written by Greg and Mary Ruth. Yet these drafts were "undated" while the drafts coming later all have dates.

Another letter dated June 26 from Universal was released that slightly amended the list to indicate that Greg and Mary Ruth's first draft done for Universal was dated February 1995 and Steven Soderbergh's draft was dated May 1995. But again, Greg and Mary Ruth submitted two drafts, the first draft, then a second draft at 98 pages submitted per the studio's edits. That is indicated in the June 2 list. Yet the draft at 98 pages in the revised June 26 list is attributed to Soderbergh. And a second draft submitted by Greg and Mary Ruth is nowhere to be found on the revised list.

Perhaps it's understandable that the arbiters may have been a little misled if this mishmash is among the paperwork sent to them.

There is something interesting to be found in the Writer Agreement – Theatrical Direct contract between Greg and Mary Ruth and Universal dated Nov. 22, 1994. Whether this had anything to do with Universal's decision to give only Story credit to Greg and Mary Ruth is not known for sure, but the fact is that Universal did stand to benefit from the duo (known collectively in the contract as Writer) not receiving a Screenplay credit. Per item b. under the "Services/Consideration" section, "If the Picture is produced, and if the Writer receives any form of 'Screenplay by' or 'Written by' credit, Universal shall pay Writer the additional sum of $125,000."

Nancy Tenenbaum estimates that by the final shooting script, "…basically all the changes that I asked Jim to make, and Steven (Soderbergh) was involved in that too, were things that they ended up spending a million three on rewrites involving other writers." The option with Greg and Mary Ruth alone was renewed at least three times over the five years the project was in development and every time they signed the new option, Universal paid them for the privilege. Add to the mix Jim Herzfeld who no doubt made sure he had a very lucrative contract with the studio, especially after word got around of Spielberg's supposed interest. Then there was Hamburg, Taylor, and Payne, and it's easy to imagine Universal perhaps balking at shelling out $125,000 more to a couple of rubes new to the industry. It's unlikely that Universal had much influence in the WGA arbitration process, but Greg and Mary Ruth not getting Screenplay credit saved the studio a good chunk of change.

The Audience Meets *Meet the Parents*

Released on Oct. 6, 2000, in North America, Universal's *Meet the Parents* grossed $28.6 million on its first weekend and remained the top-earning film for that weekend. In fact, its earnings for the weekend made it the highest-grossing film to have been released in October to that point. It would spend the next four weeks as the highest-grossing film in the U.S., and by the end of its run, it had grossed $330.4 million worldwide, very comfortably well above its production budget of $55 million.

Reviews were generally favorable.

Roger Ebert of the *Chicago Sun-Times* felt that *Meet the Parents* was funnier than Roach's Austin Powers movies because, "…it never tries too hard; De Niro in particular gets laughs by leaning back and waiting for them to come to him."

Michael Wilmington of the *Chicago Tribune* noted that the film, "…topped Variety's box-office charts surpassing $100 million in less than 24 days…" and explained, "While that wouldn't be surprising if 'Parents' were an action blockbuster, a spectacular horror movie, an event movie like 'Titanic' or another 'Star Wars' sequel, it's something of a jolt for a film so much smaller and more seemingly modest." He brought up the reason for this being the "universal chord" of its "domestic situations, psychological anguish and personal fears…" In a nice nod to the original movie, Wilmington mentions the inspiration of the silent era comedies on the movie, stating, "That's no accident: The original creators/writers of 'Meet the Parents,' Greg Glienna and Mary Ruth Clark, modeled their comedy on the silent classics."

An honorable mention no doubt very much appreciated by Greg and Mary Ruth. Especially when you have Paul Clinton of CNN.com proclaiming the film, "…one of the best comedies of this—or any other—year," thanks in part because, "Co-writers Jim Herzfeld and John Hamburg (with an uncredited assist from "Elections" (1999) Alexander Payne and Jim Taylor) have captured all the inherent angst and humorous possibilities of that situation in a well-crafted beautifully written script…"

There is some irony that the "uncredited" writers get credit in this review for helping with the humorous possibilities, many of which were first posed by Greg and Mary Ruth who aren't mentioned at all.

Kenneth Turan of the *Los Angeles Times* stated it was, "…possibly the most amusing mainstream live-action comedy since 'There's Something About Mary…'" which, considering "Mary" came out a scant few years prior, isn't really saying a lot. But Turan enthuses that the way the film "came into the world" is the real story. You see, it was "…developed the old-fashioned way…A sharp producer named Nancy Tenenbaum…acquired the rights to a short film (story credit going to Greg Glienna & Mary Ruth Clark) and hired comedy writer Jim Herzfeld to turn it into a feature." Of course, there's a bit more to the story than that, like, for example, how it was Greg and Mary Ruth who were hired to turn the original into a feature for Universal and Jim Herzfeld who was hired to tweak it, but hey, at least Turan acknowledged their "Story" credit.

Even the BBC chimed in with reviewer Neil Smith proclaiming, "There's not a weak scene in this super-funny picture."

Still, other reviewers were not quite so enthusiastic. Sam Adams of the *Philadelphia City Paper,* an alternative weekly paper at the time, fixated on how Greg's Jewishness and the Byrnes' WASPishness clashed, then stated, "But if I dwell on what might seem like a minor aspect of the movie as a whole, it's because the rest of the thing is so manifestly uninteresting." He goes on to call Jay Roach's direction "lead-footed" and states that the polygraph scene (the scene that inspired the movie poster), "…falls flat because Roach lets the pace flag enough for us to ponder the sheer unlikeliness of the situation."

Elvis Mitchel of the *New York Times* seems to have been a bit more satisfied with the film on whole yet notes, "The comedy might have been a bit sharper and less of a one-joke setup if Greg were a little less openly derided and if his concerns were amplified because he wasn't sure where he stood with Pam's family."

This of course was a misgiving Nancy, Greg, Mary Ruth, and others expressed about the remake. The Byrnes family and set of friends were often rude if not downright mean to this young man and Pam seemed more concerned with keeping familial peace than standing up for the boyfriend she claimed to love.

Jessica Winter of the *Village Voice* felt that "…director Jay Roach sabotages punch lines with setups that honk and sputter like oncoming trucks, and tends to stage Farrelly-inspired chaos only to cut away skittishly before the whole rig explodes." Which, admittedly is in itself a clunky way to make a point, but the point is nonetheless made.

Some of the reviewers were of the mind that the film was a watered-down version of *Something About Mary*. In his opinion that the characters in the film are, "…never quite allowed enough air to breathe," Peter Bradshaw of *The Guardian* invokes *There Something About Mary* (directed by the Farrelly Brothers) when he wonders, "…how the Farrelly Brothers would have developed the Focker gag." And compares the scenes with Jinx the cat to "…Farrelly animal-scenes…" and decides that the movie "…strains to come to life, but never quite makes it."

In the meantime, Jeff Vice of *Salt Lake City's Deseret News* does a full-court press in comparing *Parents* to *Mary* insisting in the first paragraph of his review, "The thinking behind 'Meet the Parents' is obvious enough—namely, trying to repeat the success of… 'There's Something About Mary'" and states that, "…it follows each laugh-out-loud scene with one that is completely—or is at least a bit—cringe-worthy."

There are those who could easily lay the very same charge on *There's Something About Mary*, but what's interesting to note about the many reviewers' obsession with *Mary* is that while they felt *Parents* was a pale imitation of the Farrelly Brothers' hit, both movies were probably in development around the same time. *Mary* just got out of the gate faster.

Still, Vice does take issue with the "…series of unfunny jokes that refer to Greg's rather unusual last name (which probably can't and shouldn't be repeated here), as well as other material that really pushes the PG-13 rating." A fair point, but one none-the-less curious coming from a fan of *There's Something About Mary* considering one of the most notable scenes in that movie concerns the male character jacking off and Mary unwittingly putting the cum in her hair thinking it's hair mousse.

Meet the Parents was nominated and did win many awards. Among them, Robert De Niro was nominated for a Golden Globe Award for Best Actor and "A Fool in Love", Randy Newman's opening song for the movie was up for an Academy Award, while the American Comedy Awards nominated the movie for Funniest Motion Picture. The film won a People's Choice Award as Favorite Comedy Motion Picture and Ben Stiller won an American Comedy Award as Funniest Actor in a Motion Picture as well as an MTV Movie Award for Best Comedic Performance.

The studio took the premise to what should have been its logical conclusion in December 2004 when it introduced us to Greg's parents in *Meet the Fockers*. Joining the ensemble of characters from the first movie were Barbara Streisand and Dustin Hoffman playing Rozalin and Bernie Focker whose liberal mentality chafes greatly against Jack Byrnes' more conservative nature. If Jim Herzfeld was fired from the *Meet the Parents* production, he and the studio must have kissed and made up since he's credited (along with John Hamburg) for the screenplay of *Meet the Fockers*, and shares a Story credit with Marc Hyman. Of course, it's also possible that his inclusion was contractual since he might have had the same clause as Greg and Mary Ruth in their contract that the writer that gets "Screenplay" credit has first dibs at writing a sequel.

Critics were not quite as charmed by the sequel as they were by the first movie. While he enjoyed the movie enough, Roger Ebert admitted that "…even if you loved 'Meet the Parents' you will only sorta kinda like 'Meet the Fockers.'"

Paul Clinton, who wrote so glowingly of the first movie, called this one "formulaic…fitfully funny" and adds "…you will find yourself laughing out loud here and there. But the freshness of the original is lacking."

Peter Bradshaw of *The Guardian* went further. "…it all looks pretty tired. The comedy isn't as bright. The embarrassments aren't as embarrassing."

Nathan Rabin was even more ruthless, stating, "'Meet the Fockers' has assembled a historic, once-in-a-lifetime cast, then stranded them in the laziest, most mercenary kind of sequel imaginable."

Little did he know that *Little Fockers* was six years away.

Still, *Meet the Fockers*, again directed by Jay Roach, found success with audiences, grossing $46,120,980 in its opening weekend and earning a total box office of $522.7 million on an $80 million budget.

Hollywood always willing to beat a dead horse, Universal tried to fire up the magic again in 2010 with *Little Fockers*, this time Roach taking on the role of producer (along with De Niro, Hamburg, and De Niro's producer partner Jane Rosenthal) leaving the directing to Paul Weitz. And this time, the screenplay was written by John Hamburg and Larry Stuckey. While not as successful as its predecessors, and hardly a favorite with the critics (Todd McCarthy of the Hollywood Reporter minced no words calling the film "focking dismal" and proclaiming it "a paycheck project for all concerned"), *Little Fockers* still managed to gross $310.7 million worldwide. The three movies combined create a billion-dollar franchise.

Not a bad figure at all for a domestic comedy.

Clearly, Greg Glienna and Mary Ruth Clark were on to something 18 years before when they wrote and produced an independent movie about a young man going to meet his girlfriend's parents and everything goes wrong.

Movie Making Is Not for the Faint of Heart

Elliot Grove has an interesting story to tell about his involvement with getting *Meet the Parents* remade into a big studio movie.

Who is Elliot Grove in this story? Well, someone Greg had never heard of until research for this book activated his name in the search engine.

Grove is the founder of the Raindance Film Festival, a yearly event held in London's West End since 1992. The festival is a celebration of the art of independent filmmaking, hosting the UK premiere of films like *Pulp Fiction* and *Momento*, and the world premiere of 1993's *What's Eating Gilbert Grape*. It has its own film school and has established The Independent Film Trust, which supports the filmmaking efforts of disadvantaged and mentally challenged youth.

In the mid-2000s, Grove compiled a list of his favorite independent movies published on the Raindance Web page and coming in at #9 is the original *Meet the Parents* (though curiously, the photo accompanying this entry is of the publicity poster from the 2000 remake). It's in his write-up for the movie that Grove alluded to the festival playing a pivotal part in the film being remade "The original version of Meet the Parents, a 16mm film, was screened at Raindance Film Festival in 1995. Emo Philips, the associate producer on the Hollywood version, used a bit of his own cash and produced this exceptional feature, which is impossible to get a hold of. The film was bought from Emo at Raindance, and he signed a terrible deal, earning only $50,000 on the deal for the picture that eventually topped the US box office in 2002. The original version was much funnier and tighter than the Hollywood version. Most of the good jokes were watered down, except the Kevin the carpenter character. (Played by Emo in the original)."

It's a fascinating write-up mainly for its inaccuracies. While indeed, one could argue that the movie was funnier and tighter than the Hollywood version, the Hollywood version nonetheless topped the U.S. box office when it was released in 2000, not 2002. He attributes the film to Emo Phillips with the production year of 1995 (four years after the actual release of the film). The film was not bought at Raindance from Emo, who doesn't even remember the festival or the incident described. The $50,000 alluded to was probably the amount of money Greg paid back to Emo after the film was optioned by Universal, but the film itself traveled on a long, and much harder road before Universal came into the picture than was implied by Grove.

And of course, Emo didn't play a carpenter character named Kevin in the original. He played a video store clerk. Kevin was the name of the boyfriend in the remake who was into carpentry.

Grove goes into it, if not in more clarification, with slightly more embellishment, on one of the pages for the festival's Website announcing the Live Ammunition Filmmakers Pitching Competition, held July 2022. According to Grove, "The first Live!Ammunition! was held in Leicester Square in what is now the VUE West End Cinema in Leicester Square in October 1994 at the 2nd Raindance Film Festival. I invited the comic Emo Phillips to pitch his new film screening two days later during the festival. It was my attempt to rustle up interest in his quirky and amusing low budget comedy. I didn't realise an acquisitions executive from Universal Studios was in the room who saw and bought world rights for the movie two days later. The film languished in the vaults for five long years when it was remade: Meet The Parents.

The original Meet The Parents has a fascinating Wiki post…"

It's an inspiring story but largely inaccurate as this book has indicated. The ironic thing about the piece is that he includes a link to the original movie's Wikipedia page in which a whole different tale on how that movie got to Universal is revealed.

It's hard to say where this story sprouted from. When contacted regarding these claims, Grove, who is a champion of the indie filmmaker, seemed very sincere in his explanation that it had been Emo Philips who filled him in on the details. But in an interview with Emo for this book, the comedian seemed mystified by the whole thing.

Perhaps the most ludicrous example of someone trying to capitalize on the success of *Meet the Parents* came a few years after the release of the Universal film in the form of a lawsuit filed on June 16, 2005, charging NBC Universal and associated agencies with copyright infringement when it came to both *Meet the Parents* and *Meet the Fockers*.

It was a move both bold and bizarre and certainly a surprise to the principal players dragged into court.

The lawsuit was filed by Joseph Ardito, a writer and would-be film producer whose production company, Chivalry Film Productions doesn't seem to have produced much of anything let alone films. In his lawsuit, Ardito claims that there were scenes, characters and situations in both Universal's *Meet the Parents* and *Meet the Fockers* that were lifted, without his permission of course, from a novel and a screenplay he wrote and copyrighted in 1998 titled *The Tenant* and *The Dysfunctionals*.

Since it seems neither the novel nor the movie was ever published or produced, it's uncertain where NBC Universal or the others named in the suit would have seen the material to plagiarize it, but Ardito had a theory and he laid it out in all its conspiratorial glory on Chivalry Film Productions' website.

So earnest is Ardito in what he views as a quest for justice that the entire Website of Chivalry Film Productions is devoted to the case. There are 14 pages on the website one can click on and every page is loaded with the same copy of Arditos venting regarding the case. Even the page for the Chivalry Store has pictures of apparel presumably for sale with the Chivalry Films logo embroidered on it, followed by the same relitigating of the case. There is no mention of any other projects Ardito may be working on.

Possibly because there is nothing else, he is working on.

He starts with a bang, claiming that not only *Meet the Parents* and *Meet the Fockers* but also *Wedding Crashers* and other movies in the industry are a product of "Stolen Federal Copyright Materials" originally created and owned by Joseph Ardito and were in fact stolen by the defendants/respondents' "Organized Crime Syndicate in a premeditated criminal scheme to deprive" him of his federal protected copyrights.

In response to the lawsuit, Greg was asked by Universal to submit an affidavit testifying to writing and copywriting the screenplay for a movie that, once made, was seen by theaters full of people in the U.S. and abroad and reviewed by major Chicago newspapers several years before Ardito's works were copyrighted. But according to Ardito, a theft ring "infiltrated the Library of Congress, F.B.I., LAPD, United States Attorney General's Office, Judicial Branch of Government and other government agencies," and he insisted that Greg's 1992 *Meet the Parents* that resided there was actually a blank tape with a case doctored up by two people at the Library of Congress to appear as if there was a real movie inside.

For Ardito it was all fraud. Steven Soderbergh (or "Sodenburg" as Ardito writes on his website), named in the suit along with the other defendants, had "through a premeditated scheme unlawfully used this plaintiff/appellants federal protected copyrights that were 'Stolen' and devised a criminal scheme with its members of the 'Organized Crime Syndicate' to pre-date a fraudulent 1991 MTP videocassette that was used as title and nothing more, in a blatant attempt of evading criminal liability, civil liability with the objective and intent of barring 'discovery.'"

John Hamburg, according to Ardito, is as connected to the "Organized Crime Syndicate" as is Steven Soderbergh and the other defendants named, which included Greg, Mary Ruth, and even

Owen Wilson who played Pam's ex-boyfriend Kevin in the 2000 remake.

Ironically one name most notably absent from the list of defendants is Jim Herzfeld.

The court found in favor of the defendants in December 2006 noting that the plaintiff's attempts to show plagiarism involved, "the most trivial and generic incidents," and again in October 2007 after the verdict had been appealed.

Such is the power of this unassuming independent movie that there are people only too happy to try to winnow their way into its history.

As for Greg, while he was frustrated at only receiving Story credit on the script for Universal, what ate at him more was his lack of access to the original film. Both he and Mary Ruth still receive residuals on the 2000 remake, but their emotional connection to that film, marred by the credit arbitration, isn't nearly as strong as their connection to the movie they put their heart and soul into making. Universal had bought the rights to the original movie...in perpetuity, a deal Greg now questions making. "I blame myself for that too. Where was my head when we were writing a contract? Why didn't I insist on getting my film...I don't remember, you know what I mean?"

It's easy to blame oneself in these situations, but both Greg and Mary Ruth were very green to the ways of Hollywood so it would have benefited from an entertainment lawyer who would have been a bit more watchful of their interests. Which they didn't have at the time. When Greg eventually replaced him with Bob Wallenstein, the new lawyer was stunned at some of the rights that Greg's former entertainment lawyer allowed to be given away to Universal.

Of course, another part of the problem was the excitement of seeing their work translated into a larger movie made them more willing to go along with it all. It was thrilling, but neither expected the direction to change as drastically as it ended up doing once the production kicked into gear. "You know when we sold it," Greg stated, "Steven Soderbergh was going to be directing it. It was going to be a lot like ours. I didn't know it would be so drastically different in tone."

When the remake came out, Greg was already living in L.A. and was able to get to the premiere. "I was happy with it. It was a good movie with Robert De Niro and Ben Stiller. I thought mine was funnier, but I was happy with it. I was glad that it did well and helped my career. I don't hate the remake. I just think there are things about it I don't like."

"I didn't see the blockbuster *Meet the Parents* until it came to the cheap theater," Mary Ruth remembered. "We were at the Patio Theater actually and I was sitting in a row in front of a young couple and in back of me was an older couple and they howled all the way through it. So...It just felt convoluted from my perspective. We really lost control when De Niro signed up because he doesn't play normal. That part of it...the whole CIA thing, it wasn't universal."

According to item B in the Special Terms clause of their contract, Greg did reserve the right to, "exploit the Short Film solely on a not-for-profit basis (e.g. film festivals and education screenings)." And indeed, the film did play at a few festivals right before and during the development of the film at Universal. This included The Edinburgh International Film Festival in 1993 and The Comedy Film Festival in Southampton, England in 1996, where Emo Philips was scheduled to appear as well. A few years after the Universal *Meet the Parents* was released, Greg and Jim Vincent flew to England to appear at a festival where clips from their movie were shown along with clips from the 2000 remake followed by a question-and-answer session with the filmmakers. This experience was particularly gratifying for the two thanks to the enthusiastic reception the audience gave to their film and the consensus that theirs was the funnier version.

But it wasn't the same thing. The fact was that his wish had always been to see his version distributed and Greg had agreed to a remake only because it seemed he'd never find a distributor for it. The indie scene has opened dramatically since the original was made and there are now many options available to him to get his movie out there. Universal, however, has it locked up tight.

The timing could have been part of it. The clause in the contract also spoke of a "Freeze Period" of four years after the theatrical release of the remake in which Universal could say "no" to any showing of the original. According to the contract, "...the Freeze Period shall be reinstated in connection with each such remake or sequel." The release of *Meet the Fockers* in 2004 came right after the Freeze Period would have ended after *Meet the Parents*. And with *Little Fockers* being released in 2010 it did not offer a lot of time to send the movie to festivals. It's uncertain why Universal agreed to allow the film in the festival that Greg and Jim attended in England since that was close to the remake's release, but it was apparent they planned on being miserly on how often it allowed this.

Universal had placed Greg in a difficult position. By denying him screenplay credit, they had made his connection to the 2000 remake less than it was. But by not allowing him easier access to the 1992 original, he was unable to exploit the one movie for which nobody could take away his credit.

Curiously, in a letter dated Aug. 8, 1997, amending the 1994 Screenplay/Option Agreement, item 3 stated that "If Universal exercises the Option [to make the film], you shall be permitted to produce and exploit one (1 feature-length, live action theatrical motion picture remake of the Short Film (i.e., a theatrical production which contains the same story and leading characters as contained in the Short Film)." There were restrictions. For example, the Short Film's remake budget could not go higher than $2,000,000. It couldn't be released earlier than six months after the release of the Universal *Meet the Parents* on videocassette, or four years from the date, Universal decided to exercise the Option. And of course, Greg's remake title was not allowed to contain the words "meet" and/or "parents." Above all, Greg would have to write and direct his remake.

This is a remarkably odd allowance for a movie studio to grant in a contract for a movie that was in development with them and illustrates that even as late as 1997, as Nancy Tenenbaum indicated, Universal wasn't sure what they wanted to do with it. It's uncertain why Greg didn't jump at the chance to produce this movie unless the sheer logistics of such an endeavor came into play. Remembering how he had to jump to get financing for the original, it's possible that he wasn't in a convenient enough position to do that again. Again, timing could have been a factor too. This was the third option renewal in two years and while they didn't want to let the property go, they didn't seem any closer to exercising their option and making the movie. Still, Greg would not want to start the process of getting the funding and beginning the filming only to have Universal come along and shut down filming because they had decided to exercise the option and Greg would need to stop mid-production because it was now in the four-year time frame.

And that all could have been exactly why Universal felt so confident to make such an offer. This option renewal may have occurred around the time Spielberg was said to be eying the script. If that was the case, then Universal may not have wanted to risk losing the property because Greg decided to take it somewhere else. So, this item may have been a way to present a sweetening of the deal all the while knowing that likely, that honey would never need to be spread.

Eventually, it wouldn't matter. A third Amendment to Screenplay Option/Purchase Agreement was sent out 13 days after the Oct. 6, 2000 premiere of the remake. In it, it states that "Paragraph 3, of the Second Amendment shall be deemed deleted in its entirety, ie Owner shall not have the right to produce and exploit one (1) feature-length, live action theatrical motion picture remake of the Short Film."

Universal strikes again.

When all is Said and Done

For being a dream factory, Hollywood has certainly broken enough of them. Even hardened veterans of the system have had their WTF-Just-Happened moments where they're left trying to understand how a project was hijacked.

It might not have been so difficult for them to stomach the decision of the WGA arbiters on credits had Greg and Mary Ruth truly only offered a story. Had they never written and filmed an independent feature and written a script for Universal. But they did. And now, bits, gags, and characters they came up with are attributed to John Hamburg and Jim Herzfeld, who is only too happy to milk the notion that he is the creator of *Meet the Parents.* "Story by" would never reflect the amount of effort and creativity Greg and Mary Ruth put into the foundation of that movie: the script.

To be fair, Greg and Mary Ruth do get residuals not only for *Meet the Parents* but sequels that are spawned from it but they're small potatoes in comparison.

And the 2000 *Meet the Parents* has gone down in history as "Jim Herzfeld's Meet the Parents" and very rarely would anyone mention the 1992 independent feature that led to a multi-million-dollar film franchise, the names of the writers of that feature mere footnotes.

The Internet has corrected that slightly. Hungry for content, Websites, and blogs discussing the Universal film often mention that it is a remake of the 1992 movie. Terminology no doubt irritating to a movie studio that has insisted, because of its length, that the 1992 original is merely a "short" and thus not an original feature film, (so of course the 2000 movie can't possibly be a remake, can it?). And if people hunt deeply enough, they may even uncover a few pirated copies of the movie uploaded to various sites. The quality isn't the finest: dupes of dupes (after all, this was a film shot on 16 mm, then transferred to video), but it is accessible for those willing to hunt.

While certainly, the result of their interaction with Universal was a disappointment, Mary Ruth tries to view the experience in a positive light. "I sort of fell into writing. Then Greg asked if I wanted to write *Meet the Parents* with him. We had no idea what we were doing. I didn't get my writing education until after that whole thing we went through with the remake. It was like it suddenly occurred to me that I had no idea what I was doing. That's when I really started putting myself through Mary Ruth Clark's structure boot camp to learn how to do this. To study how it was done."

Now a playwright with several plays under her belt, she's a Resident Playwright at Chicago Dramatists and teaches screenwriting and writing for the small screen at Second City, The Graham School at the University of Chicago, Story Studio, and Chicago Dramatists. "And I find it to be really joyful." But to her experience with *Meet the Parents*, "I tell students right off the bat, if you want to play with the snakes, you have to get a snake lawyer. This business can be gratifying, but you can trust absolutely no one, especially other writers." Then she admits, "I don't regret creating the original and watching it, and the blockbuster in a dark theater with a bunch of laughing people. The great thing is that people can DIY because there's no excuse not to now. I point out in my classes that when we shot the original MTP, the most expensive thing was the film stock. It was like 90 percent of the budget. Creators don't have that restriction anymore. In fact, my Second City students film things on their phones for final projects."

For Mary Ruth, "It was an experience. It's a party story, and I still occasionally get noticed for my performance as Fay."

For his part, Greg's experience with *Meet the Parents* has been a little bittersweet. Again, that film on his resume has helped him make the transition from gig comic to screenwriter. Fellow writers were even jealous of him because *Meet the Parents* helped Greg find an agent; not an easy thing to do in Hollywood. "I was able to get an agent which so many writers can't do when they move out here," he said. "I've had so many people go, 'How do you get an agent?' For me…you know I moved out here with a movie in production."

It helped lead him into a screenwriting career and even helped him land a job directing one of his screenplays. The film was 2006's *Relative Strangers* starring Danny DeVito and Kathy Bates as Frank and Agnes Menure, characters that might be remembered from Greg's first film *The Housewarming*. They're a little more lovable in this one, if only slightly.

At the time this book was being written, Greg had restarted his CEM Productions and was working on the finishing edits of another independent feature titled *The Road Dog*, with Doug Stanhope playing a down-on-his-luck standup comedian who gains a new lease on life, provided he can hang onto it. Written by Tony Boswell and Greg (who also directed it), the movie was financed by investors willing to take a chance on the film.

It's a chance for Greg to restart the dream he had back when National Lampoon made a deal to distribute *Meet the Parents* on video and he had hoped that would lead to the opportunity to make more films under the CEM banner. According to the company's website, Greg decided, "I've come to the conclusion that I work better when notes and outside influences are at a minimum. If I have to work with a lower budget to do my best work, that's a small price I'll have to pay."

In other words, no more worrying about option renewals and development hell. No more studio games and writers brought on at the last minute to steal the thunder from those who came before. Even more importantly, the finished product would be his with which to do what he liked. To show when he wanted to. To distribute how he liked. He'd be going back to his indie roots and would not have studio money to play with, but he would also no longer need to beg a studio for the chance to screen a film that no longer has any consequence for them.

Still, the original *Meet the Parents* is kind of like "the one that got away." The remake was released over 20 years ago. It has made a couple of decades worth of billions for Universal, as have the two sequels. Releasing the original 1992 movie back into the wild would not affect that or any future revenue the remake and sequels stand to make. If Universal had been clever, it could have added the original movie onto the DVD of the remake as a special feature. There's a whole wonderful story that predates what's typically focused on about the 2000 movie in interviews and entertainment pieces, and Universal would have been wise to celebrate that.

Remakes are released all the time without the originals being locked up in a vault. What is Universal so afraid of?

It might sound like hubris to wonder, but Greg certainly can't figure out why else they won't allow him the chance to show his film. "It's possible that they're not done with the franchise. I remember my lawyer tried to get the rights like 15 years ago, but he said it goes up very high. Whoever doesn't want it released."

According to a contract dated May 28, 2002 that remained unsigned, Palm Pictures LLC, a video distributor founded in 1997, was trying to strike a deal with Jim Vincent, Emo, and Greg to "license 'The Original Meet the Parents' for worldwide exploitation."

In a draft of an email to Universal written the previous year, anxious for his film to see the light of day again, Greg gave it his best shot in trying to convince Universal to either allow him to distribute it on his own or to have Universal include it on a DVD with the remake. He mentions the inquiries people have made after his version, as well as how helpful releasing the movie would be to his career as an independent filmmaker. Then he ends by reasoning, "Considering that we all put years of our lives into this project, it would be a tragedy if our little movie wasn't given the chance to be enjoyed on its own merits."

It was a bold attempt considering how this was about six months after the film opened in 2000 and the contract with Universal put a freeze period of four years on even showing it at not-for-profit festivals after the film was produced.

In a letter to Craig Kornblau at Universal dated June of 2002, Robert Wallenstein touches on the Palm Pictures deal and issues another request, assuring, "We understand your need to ensure that any distribution of the home video not be competitive with Universal's 'Meet the Parents' and the proposed sequel." He then offers suggestions on packaging and advertising that would help distinguish the two.

Universal's response came from Christine E. Lawton to whom Craig Kornblau had forwarded Wallenstein's request. In a letter dated June 27, Lawton cuts to the chase. "…given the existing agreement under which Universal has compensated Mr. Glienna for certain rights, as well as Universal's considerable marketing and distribution efforts on behalf of its 'Meet the Parents' release, we are unwilling to agree to consider the Palm Pictures distribution unless we can secure a form of financial compensation from such distribution that benefits Universal. We appreciate efforts to distinguish Mr. Glienna's picture from Universal's picture, but do not believe that such efforts can be entirely successful."

Very likely, that shut down that attempt. If Universal would have been content with a percentage of sales, it's likely Greg would have gladly agreed to get his movie out. But if Universal instead wanted him to pay back tens of thousands of dollars for the right to distribute his movie, it could have been a cost that Greg might not have been able to meet.

More attempts were made in June of 2006 and 2016 seemingly to no avail. His most recent attempt was in November of 2021 when he asked Nancy Tenenbaum to contact Keith Blau at Universal to see if they were willing to consider his request. Keith Blau replied to her email, "Hi Nancy—Just heard back from Business Affairs.

Unfortunately, they are not interested in licensing any rights in the Short Film back to Greg at this time. Best, Keith."

Hurray for Hollywood!

Epilogue

On September 20, 2024, the name of a small, independent film joined much larger titles like *Beetlejuice Beetlejuice, Reagan,* and *Transformers One* on the marquee of the historic Pickwick Theatre in uptown Park Ridge, IL. It was quite a homecoming for Greg Glienna who, beloved cat Aggie in tow, returned to his hometown a week before for a few months of enjoying family and friends. He also arrived with a plan.

For thirty years, Glienna watched Universal's *Meet the Parents* continue as a hot product while his film, the film that started it all, was all but lost to obscurity. Memories shared for the publication of this book deepened his frustration that his movie wasn't better known. He decided to make one more effort to get his film out there. First, at the Pickwick, later distributed on streaming platforms.

While still in Los Angeles, Greg contacted the manager of the Pickwick Theatre and arranged to have his *Meet the Parents* shown for a week. The old 16 mm print that Jim Vincent had would need to be cleaned up and brightened, and the audio more defined, but he hoped the box office would be able to cover that cost. There was also a plan to produce a trailer to be shown during the interviews that he would be taking part in thanks to publicist Danielle Garnier.

The next step would be to find a distributor to get the film up on streaming platforms once the run at the Pickwick was done. Perhaps spring of 2025.

As he made the rounds of podcast and radio interviews Danielle had arranged for him, including an interview on the WGN Morning Show, which featured his old pal Mike Toomey, Greg was fully aware of the sword hanging over his head. He had never obtained Universal's permission to do any of this.

As discussed in this book, Universal Studios owned the rights to the original film and was very picky about allowing Greg to show it. On rare occasions, he was allowed to show it at film festivals, but Universal's contract with him was clear that he would need their permission to show it, and he was not to make money off the film. Two rules he broke not only with the Pickwick run but also by his decision to get it up on streaming platforms.

It had been over 30 years. Would Universal still be petty enough to cause him trouble regarding this latest venture? But Universal was a major Hollywood studio. They'd shown their pettiness before.

"The reality that I had no right to release the film hit me," Greg admitted. "I was testing the waters to see if they would stop me. If not, I would feel more confident about getting it up on streaming."

To ease some of the risk, Greg requested that the theater bill the movie as *The Original Meet the Parents*, which technically it is.

When asked why he didn't arrange a small tour of area theaters with the movie, Greg stated, "I only wanted to do this theatrical showing to make enough money to pay for the transfer to digital and the trailer for streaming."

He couldn't deny how great it felt to see his baby on the big screen again. "I went to one of the showings and asked the person at the ticket counter what theater it was playing in. She said it was in theater four. I went into that theater and my heart sank cause there were only like 10 people in the theater. Then I saw that that theater was showing Beetlejuice Beetlejuice. I went into Theater 5 where my movie was showing and while it wasn't packed, there were more people than Theater 4."

A Q&A featuring Greg, Jim Vincent, and Mary Ruth Clarke was scheduled after the 7 p.m. opening night showing. Clarke was unable to attend, but Greg and Jim Vincent were there with a moderator. Greg did experience some preshow jitters when he checked the attendance during the week. By Wednesday of its opening, it was booked in the smaller theater and there were only 5 tickets sold online. A bit concerning. As time went on, though, the situation changed dramatically. On Sept 20, the movie was moved to Theater 3 which held 90 seats. A few hours later, the movie was moved to the 220-seat Theater 4. Sales were looking up, undoubtedly helped by last-minute postings on the local Park Ridge Facebook pages as well as the Maine South High School page which included many "Good Luck, Greg" responses from fellow alumni.

Unfortunately, it was discovered that the company that had handled the transfer didn't do the best of jobs, and Fay's grand singing scene at the end warbled up and down. Still, from the feedback, it was a successful night. And for a 30-year-old small-budget movie, it had a pretty good run for the week.

The movie industry has changed dramatically over the decades. The Covid years were a big hit. Some movie chains went under, others weathered the storm. But there are many factors as to why theater seats aren't being filled the way they might have been even in the 2000s. The digital revolution has had a hand in that. Going to the movies used to be an event. Streaming now allows movies to be instantly screened in the comfort of one's home. Trick out your living room with the latest in big screen and big sound technology, and it's almost as good as being in the theater. Cost is a factor as well. Streaming a movie in the comfort of your home may cost up to $30 for the entire family. But if you have a family of four, theater tickets alone would be even more. Big blockbuster movies that look great on the big screen have a decent shot. But the quieter dramas and comedies, movies that can be watched with as much affection on TV, aren't quite so fortunate with ticket sales, so they're less likely to be green-lighted by movie studios.

"I just know it's really hard to get people to leave their homes and go to see a movie," Greg said with some regret. The man who was adamant that his movie be seen in a theater with a group now understands that if his movie is to be seen at all, it might need to be available on streaming.

Which is where we leave the tale. If all goes well, by 2025, *The Original Meet the Parents* will be streaming on a platform near you. If Greg has poked the bear too much, Universal might put the kibosh on his sharing his original movie anywhere. Ever.

But, as has been the question for 30 years, when does Universal's reach end? Universal took an IP and made billions off it. The 2000 *Meet the Parents* ended up making $330 million. That doesn't include what each sequel has made. Greg Glienna and Mary Ruth Clarke got a taste of that, but not nearly as much as if they had been given the "Written by" credit they deserved.

At what point does Universal say, "You know what, this little fish isn't worth our time anymore" and let the guy have his movie back? It's perhaps even conceivable that Greg's movie will encourage traffic to Universal's movie, which is itself 24 years old and available on at least 10 streaming platforms.

There is enough room in this world for the original *Meet the Parents* and the remake. The question is, will Universal think so?

Time will tell.

The End